imagine your world in clay

MAUREEN CARLSON

NORTH LIGHT BOOKS
CINCINNATI, OHIO
www.artistsnetwork.com

09 08 07 06 05   5 4 3 2 1

Carlson, Maureen
    Imagine your world in clay / by
Maureen Carlson.
        p. cm.
    ISBN 1-58180-634-5 (alk. paper)
    1. Polymer clay craft--Juvenile
literature. I. Title.

    TT297.C43 2005
    731.4'2--dc22

        2004061739

Editor: David Oeters
Cover Designer: Stephanie Strang
Interior Designer: Marissa Bowers
Layout Artist: Donna Cozatchy
Production Coordinator: Robin Richie
Photographers: Val Daniels, Maureen
            Carlson, Christine Polomsky,
            Al Parrish and Tim Grondin
Photo Stylists: Jan Nickum and Nora Martini

METRIC CONVERSION CHART

TO CONVERT	TO	MULTIPLY BY
Inches	Centimeters	2.54
Centimeters	Inches	0.4
Feet	Centimeters	30.5
Centimeters	Feet	0.03
Yards	Meters	0.9
Meters	Yards	1.1
Sq. Inches	Sq. Centimeters	6.45
Sq. Centimeters	Sq. Inches	0.16
Sq. Feet	Sq. Meters	0.09
Sq. Meters	Sq. Feet	10.8
Sq. Yards	Sq. Meters	0.8
Sq. Meters	Sq. Yards	1.2
Pounds	Kilograms	0.45
Kilograms	Pounds	2.2
Ounces	Grams	28.4
Grams	Ounces	0.04

About the author

When Maureen Carlson begins a Storyclay™ Telling event, the first thing she has the audience do is reach in their back pockets for their imaginary storytelling hats. They put on the hats, reach inside and pull out a handful of imagination. They inspect it, stuff it in their mouths, chew it well and then swallow it down. Ahhh.

Maureen's Storyclay™ Telling began at the Minnesota Renaissance Festival, where she had a shop and sold her clay Wee Folk from 1979 to 1991. However, the Storyclay™ Telling had its roots even further back, when Maureen was a little girl growing up in Elsie, Michigan. Her mother, AnaBel, was a storyteller. AnaBel, or Farmer Pete's Wife, used artistic license (at least that's what the family said!) to write a weekly farmer's wife column for six central Michigan county papers. Imagination was cherished in their household.

This belief in the value of creativity led Maureen to a career in education; first in the public schools in Berea, Ohio, and then to Maureen Carlson's Center for Creative Arts in Jordan, Minnesota (www.maureencarlson.com). Maureen and her husband Dan opened the Creative Center in 1999. Besides teaching and writing books, Maureen also designs products for the gift and craft markets, including a line of Designer Push Molds for AMACO.

Maureen is the author of *Clay Characters for Kids*, *How to Make Clay Characters* and *Family and Friends in Polymer Clay*, all from North Light Books.

Dedication

I dedicate this book to all you little kids out there, whether big or small, who go through life being a little different. Maybe you have more curiosity, more energy or more questions. Maybe you have bigger glasses, bigger ears or bigger teeth. Maybe this book will help you imagine yourself into a world where you fit just right! Along the way to this imaginary world, maybe you will learn the joy and humor that comes with just being you. No one else sees the world exactly the way that you do. We are all a little different. That's what makes this world so much fun.

Acknowledgments

Many thanks to the people at North Light Books, who make my work look so good. Thank you to David Oeters, the editor of this book, who has the patience of a saint. Thank you also to book designer Marissa Bowers who added her own special flavor to the book. My hand models, Sammy Leonard and Nora Hamer, deserve applause for their cheerfully working under hot lights in the middle of a warm Minnesota spring and summer. Gratitude also goes to Valarie Daniels who stepped in as my Design Assistant in the middle of this book. Valarie, your ability to focus in on the task at hand is much appreciated!

TABLE OF contents

Note to adults

ADULT SUPERVISION NEEDED

Most children find polymer clay easy to use. However, an adult must closely supervise baking the clay, and should be available should the child have a question or need assistance as they work on the projects in the book.

GETTING STARTED

✧ Read pages 8 and 9 with the children to be sure they understand the safety precautions and helpful tips for using polymer clay.

✧ Help children understand they need to wash their hands thoroughly after handling polymer clay. Some clays will stain hands. If possible, make available a box of disposable alcohol-free wipes for easy cleaning of hands.

✧ If possible, choose an area for clay work that is uncarpeted. Protect painted and varnished surfaces and carpeted areas from unbaked clay.

✧ Be sure the children have a set of tools that are just for polymer clay and art projects. Once a tool, such as a rolling pin or a knife, is used for polymer clay, it should not be used again for food.

✧ Mixing colors of polymer clay is part of the fun, but helping your child understand color-mixing principles on pages 10 and 11 will result in less clay waste and happier results.

✧ Polymer clay doesn't dry out, but it will stay cleaner if you store each color separately in plastic bags. Store clay at room temperature away from high-heat sources, such as heating ducts and direct sunlight.

Throughout the book, you'll find other *Notes to adults* with additional information. Please take a moment to read over these sections to help the children have a higher level of success with the projects. Your involvement then becomes an important part of the creative experience.

tip

BAKING POLYMER CLAY

✧ Bake clay projects on a ceramic tile, cookie sheet or aluminum pan. Insulated pans help protect the bottom of projects from scorching, especially if the oven has hot spots. Lining the pan with white paper, baking parchment, aluminum foil or index cards help keep your pans clean.

✧ An adult should always supervise when baking clay. Follow the directions that come with the clay. Use a regular oven, convection oven or toaster oven, but not a microwave. Most clays are baked at 265° to 275°F (129° to 135°C), depending on the brand of clay. A separate oven thermometer is recommended to ensure the oven is at the proper temperature.

✧ Unbaked clay is weak and may break. Overbaked clay may scorch. If the clay scorches, open a window to remove the fumes.

✧ Baked clay can have unbaked clay added to it, and then be baked again. This is useful for adding details. However, care must be used because some clays scorch more easily than others. If the clay starts to turn brown, remove it from the oven.

✧ When baking is finished, turn off the oven, open the door and let the project cool in the oven. Be very careful when you remove the project from the oven. Hot clay is very fragile.

✧ Polymer clay hardens to a matte finish. For a glossy surface, paint the project with a matte or glossy lacquer. Test the varnish before coating the entire project, as some varnishes remain sticky and will not dry on polymer clay.

Your World in clay

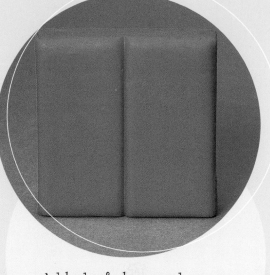

A block of clay can become more than just a block of clay.

It could be a carrot.

It could be a kangaroo.

Add a few more colors to that block of clay...

It could be a car.

... and you can imagine your whole world in polymer clay!

Getting started

Playing it safe

Making things with clay looks like fun, doesn't it? Before opening that package of clay, read these two rules:

 Don't eat clay.

 Don't burn clay.

These two rules seem very simple, and they are. But sometimes they are easy to forget, even for adults. We may accidently put tools or fingers in our mouths, or we may get distracted and leave something in the oven too long.

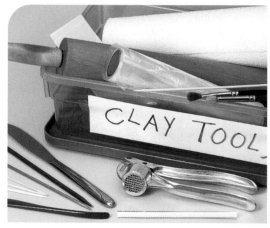

CLAY TOOLBOX ⬆

There are many tools you can use with clay, but once they are used with clay, don't use them again for foods. Keep clay tools in a special can or box, so your tools and supplies are ready when you work on a project. You can use almost anything with clay, but here's a list of some tools you might find useful.

- ⁕ clay roller
- ⁕ dull knife
- ⁕ wooden tool set
- ⁕ knitting needle
- ⁕ drinking straw
- ⁕ empty pen shaft
- ⁕ paintbrushes
- ⁕ toothpicks

Some projects call for a blunt tool. A dull knife, a knitting needle and a wood tool set will all work for such projects, depending on the size of the project. Use a smaller tool for smaller projects.

CLAY SURFACE ➡

Work with clay on a surface that is just for clay, such as a tray or a wooden cutting board, and not on something that you might use with food. Plastic-coated freezer wrap, held down with tape, is good for protecting your tabletop. Always clean your hands well after using clay. Moist towelettes make cleaning your hands simple.

NOTE TO ADULTS

There is always a safety risk when using ovens, so supervision is recommended. Burning clay not only smells badly, it ruins the project. Keep paper pieces away from the heating coils or elements in the oven. Paper does not burn at 265° to 275° F (129° to 135° C), but heating elements themselves may get hotter than that. See page 5 for more information and safety tips for using clay.

PREPARING CLAY ⬆

Polymer clay must be warmed and kneaded to make it soft and ready to use. This is called conditioning the clay. Warm the clay in your hand for a few minutes, squeeze, roll it around, then twist it until the clay is soft. Conditioning polymer clay also makes it stronger. For mixing old or crumbly clay, see the *Note to adults* at the bottom of the page.

BAKING CLAY ⬆

Polymer clay does not get permanently hard until it's baked in the oven. Have an adult help bake your clay projects. Follow the directions on the clay package for exact baking times and temperatures. If possible, use a separate oven thermometer to check your oven for accuracy. Bake your clay projects on a ceramic tile or baking pan.

PROPPING PROJECTS ⬆

Polymer clay gets soft in the oven. Prop your pieces up with index cards, or lean them against a ceramic coffee mug so they won't tip over when baking.

⬅ FINISHED PROJECTS

Once baked, your polymer clay piece is permanent. You can even wash it. Baked polymer clay is slightly flexible, especially if it is thin.

NOTE TO ADULTS

If you are conditioning a lot of clay, you may want to purchase a food processor that will be used ONLY for polymer clay. The food processor won't completely mix the clay, but it will chop and warm it so the clay is easier to knead. If your clay is crumbly, it might be old. To recondition old clay, add a softer clay or mix quick-kneading medium into the clay. Roll the softer clay through the crumbs to pick them up, then mix.

Working with clay

You don't have to hurry when you use polymer clay because it doesn't air dry. You can even leave a project overnight and come back to it another day. This means that you can change your artwork over and over again until you decide to bake it. Clay does get harder, though, once it gets cold.

SEPARATING COLORS

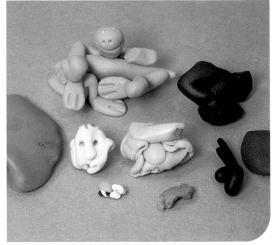

1 A polymer clay project can be made of many different colors of clay.

2 The boy on the turtle and the boy on the truck were made with exactly the same colors of clay, but see how they look different?

3 If you do decide to start over on a project, you could choose to separate the colors of clay. This would give you almost exactly the same clay with which you started, and nothing's been wasted.

SQUISHED COLORS

1 If you squish your project into a tight ball, the colors will be hard to separate.

2 If you decide to mix the squished colors together, first you will get interesting stripes. If you keep mixing, the clay will turn all one color. Often this mixed color will be gray or brown.

Mixing colors

Learning how to use a color wheel will help you mix clay in a way that creates the new colors you want.

When mixing new colors, start with just a pinch of each color of clay. Lay the colors next to each other, then keep twisting and mixing until you have a new color of clay. If you like the color, you can mix more clay. If you don't like the color, you haven't spoiled much clay and you can try again.

← COLOR WHEEL
In this color chart, the dragonflies in the middle represent the primary colors, which are red, yellow and blue. This chart shows how all other colors are made by mixing different amounts of these three colors. Flying out between the red and yellow dragonfly is one with an orange body. Orange is made by mixing together red and yellow. Look at the other two dragonflies. Mixing yellow and blue makes the dragonfly with the green body. Mixing red and blue makes the purple dragonfly. The circles on the outside show what happens when you mix different amounts of the three primary colors. You get different shades of red, orange, yellow, green, blue and purple.

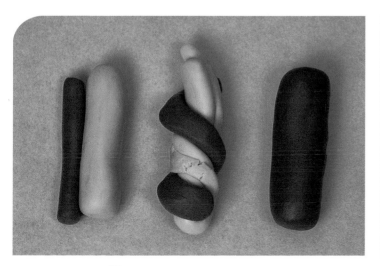

DULL COLORS ⬆
Colors that are opposite each other on the color wheel will usually be darker and duller when mixed together.

BRIGHT COLORS ⬆
Colors next to each other on the color wheel will be quite bright when mixed together.

Seeing shapes

Everything in the world is made up of shapes. Once you learn to SEE and MAKE simple shapes, you can combine those shapes to create almost anything in your world. Learning to make simple shapes is the first step to imagining your world in polymer clay. Combining those simple shapes together creates more complex shapes, such as people.

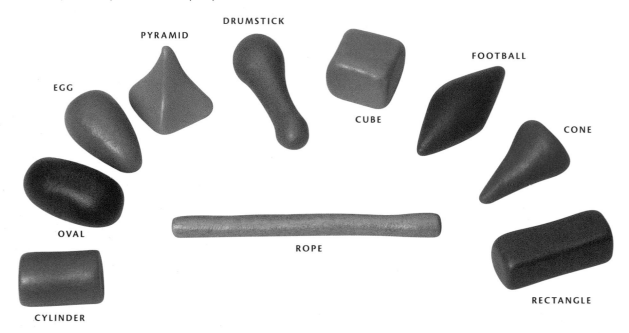

DRUMSTICK

PYRAMID

EGG

FOOTBALL

CUBE

CONE

OVAL

ROPE

CYLINDER

RECTANGLE

IT'S A BIRD!

Two simple shapes that are used a lot are balls and teardrops. This bird is made up of ball and teardrop shapes. There are three balls and six teardrops of clay. Can you find them all in the picture? Notice that the bottom of the teardrops flatten when they are pressed against the bird's head.

IT'S A DOG! ⬆

Even simple ball and teardrop shapes can be combined in many different ways. This dog is made up of the same shapes as the bird: three balls and six teardrops. Can you think of other ways to combine these shapes?

Finding shapes

Usually more than one or two shapes are used to make an animal or a person. Twelve of the shapes from page 12 are used to make this sculpture of Stan the man, Fran the cow, Jen the hen and her henhouse. Can you find all twelve shapes?

STAN, JEN AND HER HENHOUSE 🔼

If you look carefully, you can see many shapes in this picture.
STAN: two ovals, eight balls, four eggs, one cone and six ropes. You can find many more ropes in his hair!
JEN: five balls, one cone and one teardrop.
THE HENHOUSE: one rectangle, one cube and one pyramid.

BLENDING SHAPES

If you blend the lines between shapes, the figures look more real and less like a cartoon. Notice how the ears and the football-shaped eyelids on Fran the cow are blended into the head. Can you see that the shapes are still footballs and eggs, even after they are blended?

FRAN THE COW 🔼

Fran the cow has five ropes, one big rectangle, one drumstick, six balls, two eggs, one cylinder (her neck) and two footballs (her eyelids).

Making shapes

On the previous pages you learned to see and recognize shapes. Now you're going to learn to make those shapes. First, look at these funny pencil puppets.

Each pencil puppet was made using one of the basic shapes from page 12. Once the shape was made, all that was needed to complete each puppet was the addition of eyes, a nose, a mouth and a pencil. Do you recognize the shape used for each of the pencil puppets?

Turn to page 20 to learn how to make your own pencil puppets.

tip

THE BALL
You can make many things with the ball shape, like heads, the sun, the full moon and eyes.

1 If you press too hard when rolling a ball, the clay will be flat. If you don't press hard enough, the clay will be wrinkled. Practice going round and round until you get the ball just right.

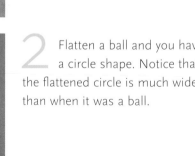
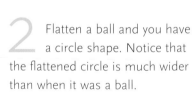

2 Flatten a ball and you have a circle shape. Notice that the flattened circle is much wider than when it was a ball.

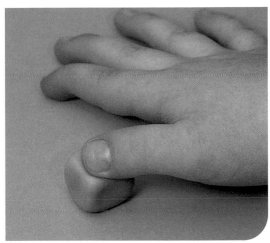

← THE CUBE

Houses, trucks and cartons are all things that can be made with the cube.

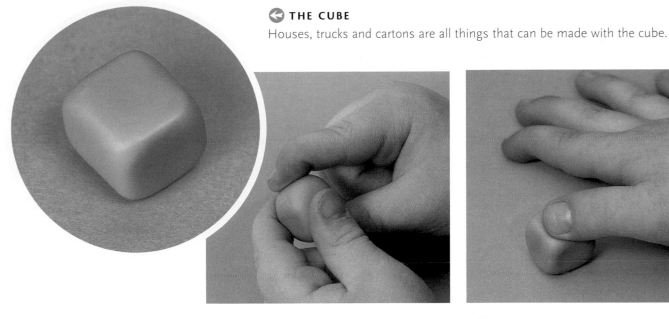

1 Turn a ball into a cube by pressing it between four fingers. Turn the cube and press it again the opposite way. This makes all six sides of the cube flat.

2 To make the sides even flatter, press all six sides against the table.

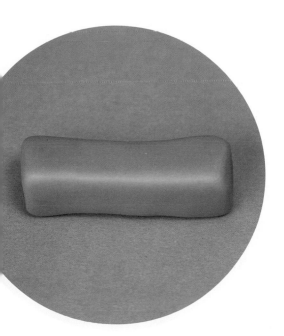

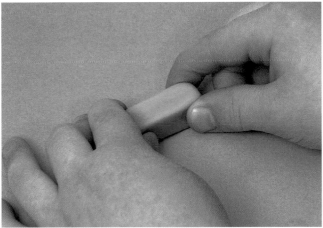

1 Stretch the cube into a longer shape by pulling along two opposite sides. This makes a rectangle.

2 Press the rectangle shape to flatten it. A flattened rectangle is a useful shape we will often use in this book.

THE RECTANGLE ↑

You can make doors, books, windows and wagons with the rectangle.

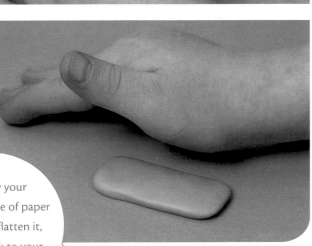

If you lay your clay on a piece of paper before you flatten it, it won't stick to your work surface.

tip

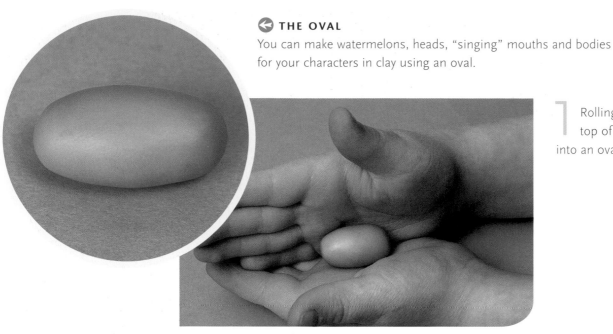

THE OVAL

You can make watermelons, heads, "singing" mouths and bodies for your characters in clay using an oval.

1 Rolling across the top of a ball turns it into an oval.

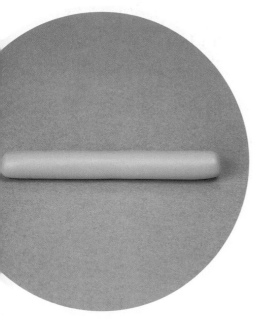

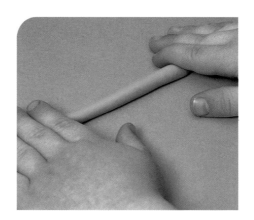

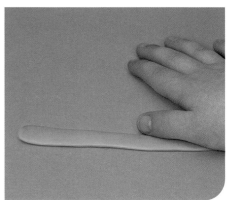

THE ROPE ⬆

Snakes, arms, legs and hair are just a few of the things you can make with the rope shape.

1 To make a rope, start by making an oval, but keep rolling until the oval is long enough to stretch. To make the rope smooth, stretch it gently by spreading your hands and fingers apart as you roll.

2 If you press hard on the rope and flatten it, you will have made a clay ribbon.

THE CYLINDER

If you make a very short rope, by cutting off the ends, for example, you've made a cylinder.

1 Roll your hand or finger against one side of the ball to create an egg shape.

2 If the egg gets too pointed, pat the pointed end down.

THE EGG ⬆

An egg shape can be used to make heads, bodies, noses and ears for your clay characters.

⬅ **THE DRUMSTICK**

Try making animal heads, bodies, guitars and vases with the drumstick.

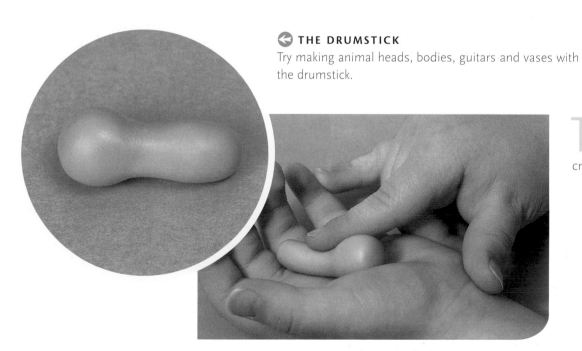

1 Roll one finger against the middle of an egg to create a drumstick.

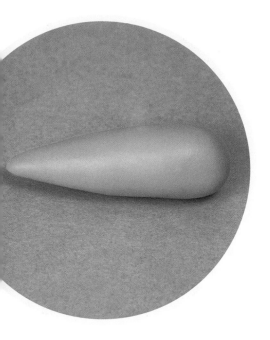

◀ THE TEARDROP

Flower petals, wings, beaks and leaves can be made with the teardrop shape.

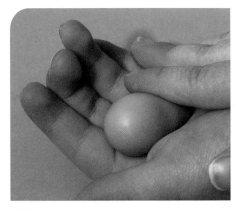

1 Roll harder against one side of the ball and you can turn an egg into a teardrop.

2 You might need to smooth out your teardrop by rolling it in your palm to get a nice shape.

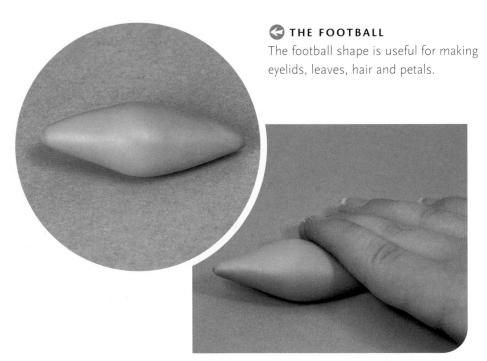

◀ THE FOOTBALL

The football shape is useful for making eyelids, leaves, hair and petals.

1 Roll your hand or finger against the other end of a teardrop to turn it into a football.

FLATTENED SHAPES

You will find flattened shapes very useful in creating a world of clay. The flattened cone looks like a triangle, and the football looks like a diamond. What other shapes can you make by flattening clay?

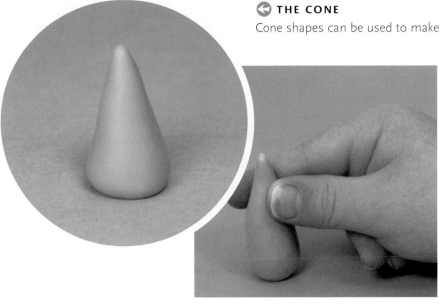

⬅ THE CONE

Cone shapes can be used to make beaks, horns and carrots.

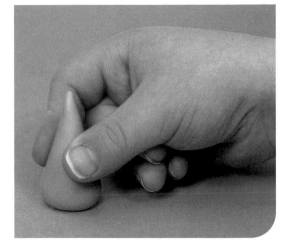

1 To create a cone, press the larger end of a teardrop against a flat surface.

2 Press a little harder and smooth out the sides to finish the cone.

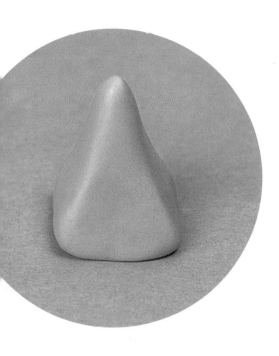

THE PYRAMID ⬆

The pyramid shape can be used to make houses and roofs.

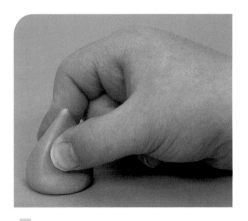

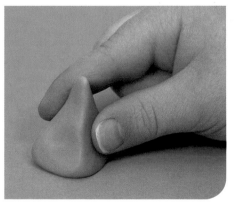

1 To turn a cone into a pyramid, press the sides of the cone between your fingers. First pinch one way, then turn the cone and pinch again.

2 Make sure the sides of your pyramid are straight and the edges are even.

Pencil puppets

Even simple shapes can be turned into fun projects if you use your imagination. When I looked at the twelve basic shapes on page 12, I wondered what would happen if I turned each one into a character by adding just eyes, a nose and a mouth. Would they need a body or arms and legs in order to look finished? Turn to page 14 to see what you think.

To make each puppet, follow these steps:

1. **Give your clay shape a face by following the steps for making eyes and mouths. The noses are just balls of clay pressed in place.**

2. **Press a wood pencil into the bottom of each face. Make sure not to damage the face.**

3. **Bake the puppet by following the directions on the package of clay.**

NOTE TO ADULTS

Be careful when baking the pencil puppet in the oven. Some pencils are made of wood and glue that may soften in the oven. To keep your pencil from warping or bending in the heat, make the shape of your puppet, press it onto the pencil and remove it, leaving a hole in the clay. You might also bake the puppet on a wood dowel that is the same size as the pencil. This would be a good idea for the rope puppet. Bake the clay following baking directions on the package of clay and on pages 5 and 9. After the puppet has cooled, press it back onto the pencil. You may have to add thick white glue to hold it in place.

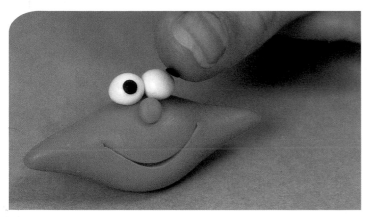

MAKING EYE"BALLS" ⬆

To make simple eyes, roll two white balls and two tiny black balls. Press the white balls in place first. Next, put the black pupils onto the white balls. To keep the eyeball round, slighlty flatten the black pupil on your finger before adding it to the eye.

⬇ MAKING SIMPLE MOUTHS

Cut away one edge of a plastic drinking straw. Press it against the clay to create a half moon shape that looks like a smiling mouth. Curve the plastic even more by pressing the ends together as you push it into the clay to make many different mouth shapes with just one piece of plastic.

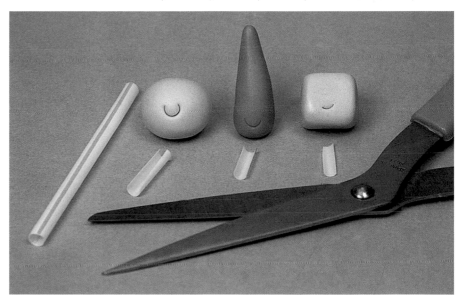

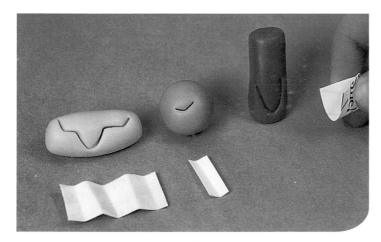

MORE MOUTHS TO MAKE! ⬆

For a larger mouth, cut a piece of thin plastic from the lid of a deli carton. Bend the cut piece of plastic over the edge of a knife to curve it. Bend it in several places to make it wavy. Experiment by using thin or thick plastic.

Turn to page 27 for more tips on making mouths. Turn to page 32 for more information on making eyes.

tip

imagine the people
in your world

What do the people look like who live in your imaginary world? When you create clay people, you get to decide lots of things about those people. You get to decide their color, their shape, how tall they are, how skinny they are, the clothes they wear, what their hair looks like, or even if they have any hair.

On these pages I'll show you how to make a few of the people who live in my clay world. I invite you to change the characters any way you like so they fit into your clay world. You can change the color of their skin or the size of their nose and ears. And you can certainly change their expression.

You may not think you'll be able to make clay people, but you've already learned how to make the basic shapes. This will be very useful as you begin to make clay people. You'll begin this chapter by mixing colors of clay for skin. Then there are sections on making each part of the face, hands, feet and bodies. If you concentrate on one part at a time, it won't seem so hard. So, turn the page and let's begin.

Secrets to creating clay characters

You can make people by just stacking shapes of clay together, but what if you want to make clay characters that look like the real people in your family, your neighborhood or your world? What if you want to make imaginary people with funny expressions and unusual poses? Would you like to make clay characters that tell a story by how they look?

Those are the kinds of things you will learn in this part of the book.

Skin color

One of the first things you might notice about a clay character is its skin color. Because polymer clay is easy to mix, you can make clay people in any color you like, even green or blue! However, most "real" people are some color of beige or brown, ranging from a very, very pale creamy beige to a rich, dark brown.

ADD A LITTLE BLUSH

Add a little color to the cheeks, nose, knuckles and chins of your clay characters by brushing a tiny amount of makeup blush or powdered chalk onto the unbaked clay. This makes the characters look more alive! Choose a color of blush or chalk that is a little darker or brighter than the color of clay you used for skin.

STRIPED PEOPLE!

Be careful when mixing two or more colors of clay for skin. Twist and mix the clay until it is completely one color. If you stop too soon, you'll have striped people!

Creating a skin color

Decide what color you would like your clay people to be, then use this chart to help you mix a color that is just right for you.

This chart uses four colors of clay — white, beige, caramel and brown — to create seven different skin tones. Look on this chart for a color you would like to use for a character, then see what clays I mixed to create the color. You could mix them in even more combinations to create a whole range of skin colors. Which one is closest to your skin color?

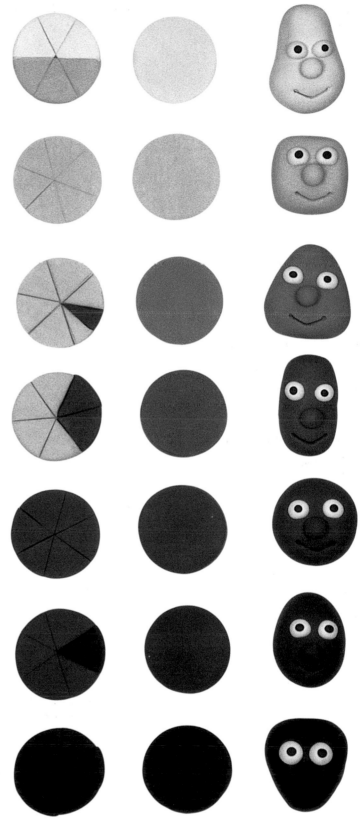

USING THE CHART

1 One way to mix clay skin colors is to make two circles of clay, one beige and one brown. Cut each into six pieces, like a pie.

2 Look on the chart to see how much of each clay you will need for a new color. Choose parts of each color circle for the new color. This one has four parts beige and two parts brown. When all six parts are mixed and twisted together, you create a new color: light brown.

The head

The head is one of the best ways to give your clay people personality. The whole face says a lot, not just the mouth! Even the shape that you use for the head of your clay character seems to change its personality.

Heads can be shaped like balls, drumsticks, eggs, triangles, ovals and cubes. When you make clay characters, head shapes can be exaggerated, as they are in cartoons. No one has a completely triangular or square head, but their head may remind us of that shape.

If you don't like the head, just squish up the clay and try another one.

CREATING A CHIN

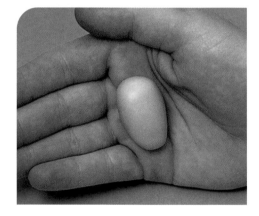

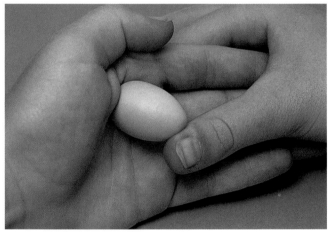

1 An egg shape is close to the shape of a real person's head, but one thing lacking is a strong chin. Roll the face section of the head from side-to-side in your hand. This will flatten the front and give the head more of a chin. If you tip the head, you will create less chin and more forehead.

2 To make the chin stick out more, press up with your thumb behind the chin.

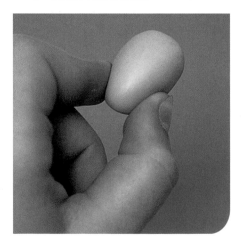

3 To add shape to the jaw, narrow the area just behind the ears by squeezing the chin gently between your fingers.

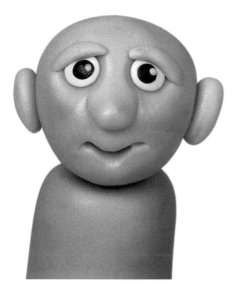 

The Mouth

The people in my family like to talk a lot! My family sings, makes faces, smiles and frowns. You can do a lot with the mouth of a clay character to create personality. There are many ways to make mouths. For some other ideas, look on page 20 for some pencil puppet techniques.

A BIG, SMILING MOUTH

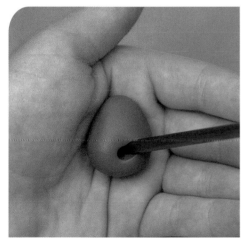 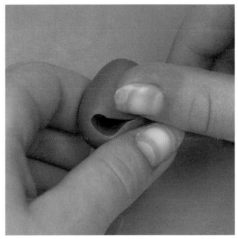 

1 Start by opening the mouth with a smooth tool, such as a knitting needle. Make the hole quite deep, then widen the mouth by rolling and pressing the tool in a smooth swing, first to the left and then to the right.

2 The mouth now looks very wide! Gently press the corners of the mouth together by pressing the cheek and chin toward each other.

3 Do the same to the other side of the mouth, then smooth the cheeks by patting and smudging the clay with your fingers. You can indent the corners of the mouth with a blunt tool, such as a knitting needle, to make the mouth look even more cheerful.

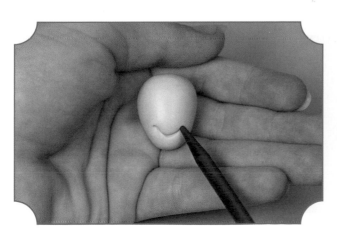

ADDING EXPRESSION

Mouths will have more expression if you indent the corners slightly. Make the mouth with a cut piece of straw, as we did on page 20. Use a knitting needle at the corner of the mouths to create the indentation, then pat and smooth to soften the indentation.

Lips

Mouths that are just pressed into the face can give the character lots of expression, but they don't have lips. It certainly isn't necessary to make lips, but aren't they fun? Adding lips makes the characters look more colorful. Each lip began as a little football shape.

1 To make lips, create two tiny football shapes out of clay (see page 18). Flatten both footballs. Press a dent in the top lip with a smooth, blunt tool, such as a knitting needle or a pointed paintbrush handle.

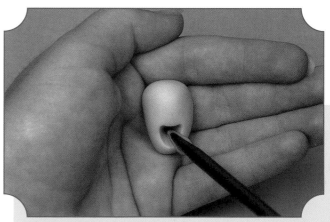

ADDING A TONGUE

If you want to add a tongue, leave the mouth wide open. Flatten a pink clay teardrop. Place it on the end of a blunt, pointed tool and press it into the mouth. Roll the tool to release the tongue, then close the mouth slightly by pressing the cheeks and chin.

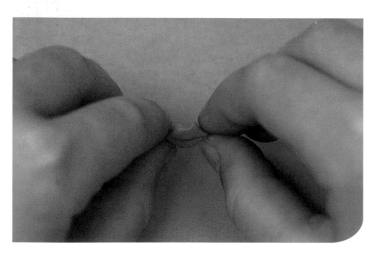

2 Lay the top lip slightly over the corners of the bottom lips. Use your fingers to press the corners together. Stretch the corners slightly, then turn them up if you want the lips to smile. Press the lips in place on the face.

Teeth

When "real" people smile or make faces, sometimes their teeth show. Sometimes it's fun to exaggerate teeth by making them very big, very small, or spaced far apart. How did you look when you lost your first tooth?

It isn't hard to make teeth, but you do have to be careful. If you get lots of fingernail marks or dirt in the white clay, your character will look like it needs a visit to the dentist!

ADDING TEETH

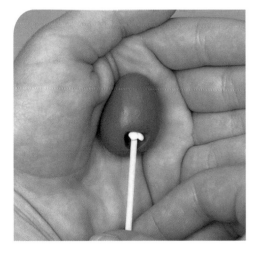

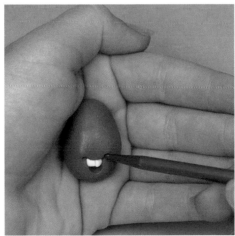

1 To make a mouth with teeth, start with an open mouth. Roll little ropes for teeth. Flatten the ropes, then use a toothpick to place the teeth at the edge of the mouth opening. Check the size of the teeth. How do they look? If they are too big or too small, remove them and make new ones.

2 To make the mouth smile, indent the corners of the mouth with a blunt, pointed tool, such as a knitting needle. You can stop here, or you can add lips over the teeth.

3 Make the lips as you did on page 28. Don't press the two lips together. Instead, pick up each one separately and press them over the edges of the mouth opening.

The Nose

Sometimes the noses in one family all look alike because we inherit the shape of our nose from our parents. Noses can be big or small, crooked or straight, turned up or turned down.

Changing the shape or size of a character's nose can really change the look of the character. Make a character, then experiment by putting different noses on the same character. Take a look at your friends and family. What kind of nose do they have?

CREATING A NOSE

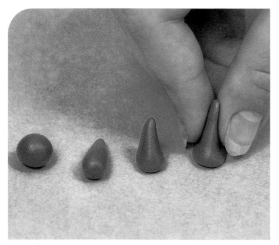

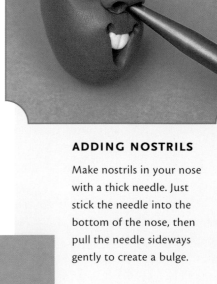

1 Simple noses can be made from balls, teardrops or cone shapes. Pinching one side of a cone will create a more realistic nose.

2 Noses can be pressed into place on the face, or you can use your finger to blend the top of the nose into the forehead.

ADDING NOSTRILS

Make nostrils in your nose with a thick needle. Just stick the needle into the bottom of the nose, then pull the needle sideways gently to create a bulge.

3 For a more realistic face, make eye sockets by rolling a round-tipped tool against the side of the nose. This creates a narrow top, or bridge, on the nose.

Ears

What about ears? I like to exaggerate the size of ears to make my characters look more whimsical.

Ears are easy to change by making them bigger or smaller, fatter or flatter. Since the clay is soft, you can curve the tops of the ears by just bending them over. You can even pinch them into a point so they look like fairy ears. Ears that are oversized may look stretched out and droopy.

Ears are easy to take off and change if you think of it as just "trying them on for size". To do this, just lay them gently against the head. Remember to press the final ears firmly in place before you bake the clay or they may fall off.

MAKING EARS

1 To make the ears, start with a ball of clay, then change it into an egg shape. Flatten the egg, then roll a round tool into one side to create a rim for the ear.

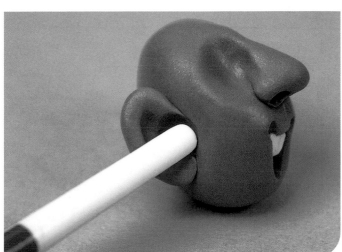

2 Place the ear halfway back on the head. Press a smaller round tool into the ear, right on the line of the ear and the head, to make the ear hole.

Rolling the round tool GENTLY along the edge of the ear and against the head will flatten, or erase, the seam.

tip

Eyes

Let's take a closer look at eyes.

Eyes are the messengers of the face. They tell you what the character is thinking and feeling. Wide open eyes show surprise. Half open eyes look sleepy. Eyes that are curved at the bottom and top look smiley. If you curve the eyelid down towards the center of the eye, your character will look grouchy.

Look in the a mirror at your own eyes? What do they say about you?

SIMPLE EYES
Plain black balls for eyes make the character look innocent or surprised. Change the size of the ball to change the look of the character. Press the balls in place on the face, or make a hole first then drop the ball in place. You can also add little dots in the center of the eye by pressing with a toothpick point.

MAKING THE EYES ALIVE!
If you add a teeny, tiny ball of white clay to the side of a black pupil, you create what looks like a reflection of light. This makes the character look more alive. Make it too big, however, and the character may look blind. This gets easier with practice.

REALISTIC EYES
The most realistic eyes start with a white ball of clay that is pressed into the face, or into a hole in the face. Add a colored ball for the iris, a black ball for the pupil and a tiny white one for the highlight. Try to make both eyes look in the same direction.

EYELIDS ⬆

If your want to make eyelids for your character, roll two tiny footballs. Flatten them, then place them over the top of the eyes.

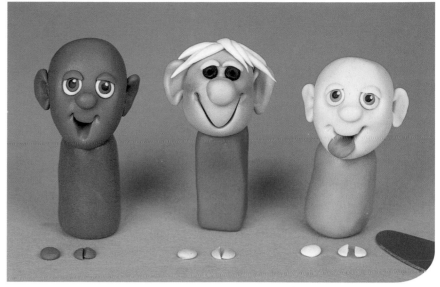

EYELID PERSONALITY! ⬆

Eyelids can give a character personality. Make a ball of clay and flatten it. Cut the flattened circle in two, and place a half over each eye. Droopy eyelids make a character look sleepy, while perky eyelids make a character look excited.

EYEBROWS ⬆

These characters have four very different sets of eyebrows.

* The grumpy character has eyebrows that are down in the center and close together.

* The surprised character has eyebrows that are up in the center and far apart.

* The worried character has eyebrows that are up in the center and close together.

* The happy character has eyebrows that are just slightly raised.

You can experiment by making different shapes of curved ropes for eyebrows.

For wispy eyebrows, carve lines in the clay with a toothpick.

tip

Hair

"Hair" today, gone tomorrow!

One of the easiest ways to make a clay character look like someone we know is to give the character the same hair color and haircut as that person. Sometimes just that one thing—the hair— will make us think of a certain person.

For inspiration, look at all the haircuts you see around you. Even people without hair can give you inspiration.

CURLY HAIR

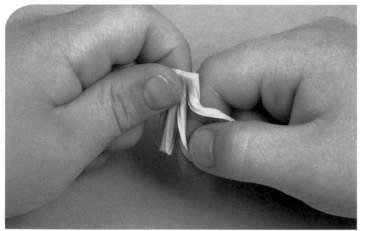

1 To make curly hair, flatten a rope of clay. Use a knife to cut strips in the clay. Pick up a section of clay, and then use your fingers to twirl each piece.

2 Press sections of curled hair to the head, starting at the back and sides. Continue until the whole head is covered.

> Hair usually is more than one color. Mix together two different colors of clay, or start with transparent clay and add color to it. To make the hair look more real, don't mix the colors completely.

tip

CLOSE CROPPED HAIR ⬆

For sculpted hair, press the hair onto the head like a helmet. Make lines in it with a toothpick or knitting needle.

WAVY HAIR ⬆

Make a rope. Cut the rope into sections. Use larger sections for larger clay characters. Make each section into a long teardrop. Flatten the teardrops. Twist or roll the teardrops slightly, and then lay the hair on the character's head. The wider end of the flat teardrop is attached to the head.

VERY CURLY HAIR

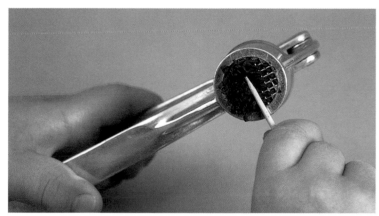

1 A garlic press makes terrific hair. Press very soft clay through a garlic press. Remove the clay by scraping across the press with the end of a toothpick.

2 Use the toothpick to press the hair onto the head. Roll the toothpick against the head to remove the clay hair from the toothpick.

Remember, once you use the garlic press for clay, it should stay in your clay box and not be used for food again.

tip

Hands

Have you ever heard of someone who talks with their hands?

Hands express feelings by their movement and position. Hands can also be used to let your clay people hold something. What they hold will give a clue about their personality. What will your clay people be doing?

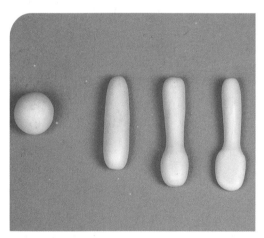

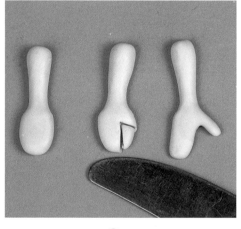

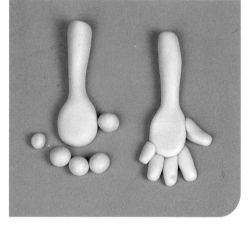

SIMPLE HANDS ⬆

For simple paddle hands, begin with a ball, then make skinny drumsticks. Flatten the large end.

ADD A THUMB ⬆

Start with a flattened drumstick, then cut out a section to create the thumb. Smooth cut edges with a finger. Stretch the thumb if it is too short or too fat.

ADD FINGERS ⬆

Make a paddle-shaped hand with a shorter paddle. Roll a tiny ball for each finger, then roll each ball into a short rope. Press the ropes to the paddle.

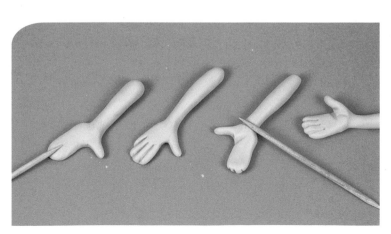

⬅ REALISTIC HANDS

Make a paddle-shaped hand with a thumb, then use a toothpick or needle to press in three lines for fingers. On the palm side, press the toothpick across the palm and wrist to shape the hand.

Feet and shoes

Have you ever looked under a crowded table at all the different feet? Just because feet are on the bottom of the body doesn't mean they should be forgotten.

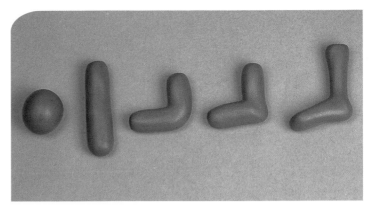

BARE FEET OR BOOTS? ⬆

To make a foot or boot, bend a rope gently. Use a quick turn (see page 49) to make the heel. Gently roll the back of the foot between your fingers to smooth it and create an ankle. You may choose to add little balls or short ropes for toes.

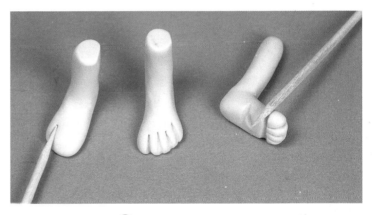

CREATING TOES ⬆

To add toes, make a basic foot shape, and then use a toothpick to press in toe lines. Turn the foot over and press a line at the base of each toe and across the center of the foot.

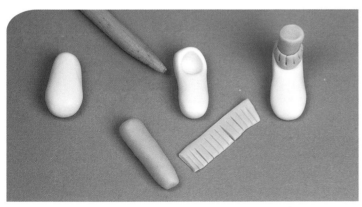

MAKING SHOES ⬆

Use different colored clay for the shoes, socks and legs. For each shoe, slightly flatten one side of a drumstick. Roll a short rope for the leg. For the sock, flatten a rope and press lines in it to make it look ribbed. Use a blunt tool to press a hole in the shoe. Wrap the sock around the end of the leg and press it in the hole. Squeeze the back of the shoe to hold the leg in place.

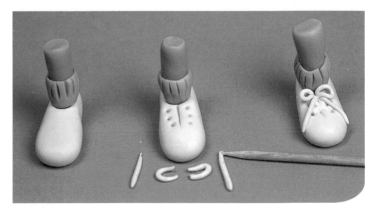

SHOELACES ⬆

Use a toothpick to poke holes in the shoes for shoestrings. Press lines between the holes so they look like your own shoe-strings. For a bow in the shoestring, roll two skinny ropes and make small loops so that the ends touch. Place them at the top of the shoe.

Poses

Once you create a character, you can bend it into a fun position! You can keep trying different poses for your character until it is baked, but polymer clay may tip over in the oven if it is not sitting or standing very, very straight. For posed characters to hold their shapes in the oven, they may need to be propped with bent pieces of cardstock or a crumpled paper towel. Since polymer clay is baked at a low temperature, paper is safe to use in the oven as a prop, as long as it does not touch the heating elements.

BENDING SHAPES
This figure began as a cone shape that was flattened slightly, then bent. She doesn't need propping because she is sitting very straight. Her arms are in her lap, so they will stay where they are even when the clay gets hot.

BEND A LITTLE MORE ➡
This figure I bent at the waist. With no toothpicks or anything inside her legs for support, the heat of the oven may cause this character to topple over. Cut and bend a piece of cardstock to fit underneath the character. Tape it together to make a little triangle. Remove the triangle when the clay is cool.

> If any of your characters isn't steady after baking, let them cool, then press a piece of raw clay to the unsteady part and bake the character again. Remember to prop the character if you bake it again.

tip

REALLY BENT!
This character is standing on his head and is supported by his arms and head. He will tip over in the oven. Cut and fold cardstock into wedge shapes for support. Hold the shapes together with paper clips, and add weight to the paper. Place the figure in the oven with the support pieces right next to him. Remove them when the clay is cool.

Armatures

Tiny characters, like the ones on page 38, can be made of solid clay. Larger characters may need a foil body armature. An armature is like a skeleton for clay figures. You can create an armature and then wrap clay around it like skin. Armatures are important for several reasons when making clay characters:

* An armature uses less clay than a solid figure.
* Using armatures helps the clay bake more evenly.
* Armatures make the characters stronger so they aren't as easy to break.

I use aluminum foil to make armatures because it isn't too expensive and it's easy to find at the grocery store. It holds its shape when crumpled, and it's safe to leave inside your clay characters.

1 Start making an armature by deciding what shape it will be. Then get a piece of aluminum foil and begin crumpling it.

2 Wad the aluminum foil up tightly so it has a smooth shape and there are no hard ridges.

3 Roll the aluminum foil on the table to create the basic shape. Shape the foil just as you would clay. If you have too much foil, unroll it and tear some off. If you need a larger armature, just add more foil by wrapping it around your basic shape.

NOTE TO ADULTS

If clay for a project is thicker than 1" (2cm), it may not bake evenly. It may even crack when it bakes. The general guideline for baking polymer clay is to bake 15 minutes for every ¼" (1cm) of thickness. If you follow this formula, a 2" (5cm) ball of solid clay might have to bake two hours in order to thoroughly bake the inside. But if you bake that long, the thinner parts of the clay sculpture may scorch. This is one reason it is a good idea to use armatures for larger clay projects.

Making characters in clay

Making clay people doesn't have to be hard. Just stack some of the shapes that you already know. Choose shapes that, when combined, look like bodies, heads, arms and legs.

When I'm making characters, I first play with the shapes to see what looks good together. Then I move the shapes around in order to see what my clay character might be doing. With clay, it is easy to take the pieces apart and start over if I don't like how they look.

Start with some simple characters. Then, as you get comfortable working with clay, you can add more complicated parts to your characters, such as teeth (page 29), hands with fingers (page 36) and shoes with shoelaces (page 37). Later in this book, you will learn to make many more kinds of clothing, such as different kinds of hats (page 56) and uniforms (page 62).

Look on pages 14-19 for instructions on how to make the basic shapes you'll use to create clay characters.

tip

Small Characters

You can make clay characters any size you want, but start with small characters. See how small you can make one of them! You can make many small characters with just a little clay.

James

James looks like he's singing a song, or is he just yawning? When I make clay people, sometimes I give them a story. If I were going to tell a story about James, I might pretend that he is singing from the top of a hill in Tennessee. He is singing way up there because he isn't very good at it, and he's afraid to let others hear him. Silly James, he doesn't know that songs and singing are all about joy and sharing.

Check the size of the body shapes by putting them next to the body to see if they fit. If one body shape seems too big or small, just add or take away a bit of clay, then roll the shape into a ball and start over.

tip

CREATING JAMES

1 First, choose the colors of clay you will use. Warm the clay between your hands. Condition and mix the clay until it's smooth and pliable. It's easiest to start each shape as a ball. For James, you need six tiny red balls, one large beige colored ball and five smaller beige colored balls, five purple and two green colored balls. Lay out all the clay balls next to each other to make sure the size and color is right. It doesn't look like James yet, but you can see him beginning to take shape!

2 Roll each ball of clay into the shape for the body part. James has a rectangular box for his body, ropes for his arms and legs, and eggs for his shoes, hands and head. His ears, eyes and nose are balls. His hair is made of flattened footballs. If you like, you can also create eyelids with flattened footballs. Attach the pieces to create the face and use a knitting needle to create the mouth.

tip

Sometimes when you press the head onto the body, you may forget that it already has a face. You may pinch too hard and distort it. The head will be easier to add to the body if you use a toothpick to poke a hole through the neck and into the bottom of the head. Then place the head and neck onto the toothpick that's in the body.

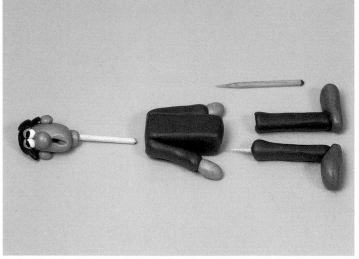

3 Press the body parts together, using a piece of toothpick to attach the head and neck to the body. Standing characters may need a toothpick in each leg to keep them from collapsing in the oven. The toothpicks should be long enough to fit through the leg and into the body. If the toothpick is too long, break off a piece. Be careful, as toothpicks can be very sharp.

4 Prop standing characters while baking because polymer clay will turn soft when it gets hot. An old ceramic mug and some twine works well. Place a piece of paper between the character and the mug. Bake the clay with adult supervision. Follow the directions on the clay package for exact baking times and temperature. After baking, let the figure cool before you touch it.

Susan

Susan is off to work today in her shop, where she sells some of the best candy you'll find in town! She's an easy project to make. Using a cone for her skirt helps her to stand.

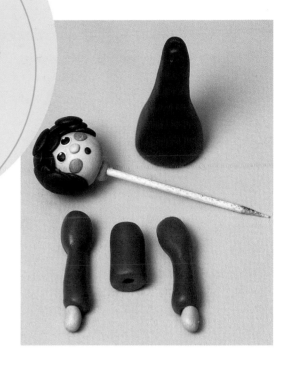

CREATING SUSAN

To make Susan, stack together a cone and a cylinder to make her skirt and body. Two drumsticks make her arms, with an egg for each hand. Use a ball for her head. To hold her head in place, press a piece of toothpick into her body. Attach her head to her body with a small ball of clay for her neck. Her eyes, nose, mouth, cheeks and hair are all balls as well. All the balls on her face and head (except for her nose) are flattened when they are pressed in place.

Antonio

Poor Antonio is worn out from all the work he's been doing! Give Antonio something to sit on. It could be a rock, chair or bed (as shown on pages 64-69). But it could also be just a bench made out of a block of clay.

CREATING ANTONIO

For Antonio, use a ball for his pants and an egg for his shirt. Use a toothpick to attach the pants, body and head together. His lower legs are ovals, and his upper legs are cylinders. The two shapes should be pressed together at the knee, creating a bend. His shoes, ears and hands are eggs, and his head, nose and neck are balls. His hair started as a flattened ball. Before baking Antonio, turn or tilt his head in to make him look like he is thinking or listening.

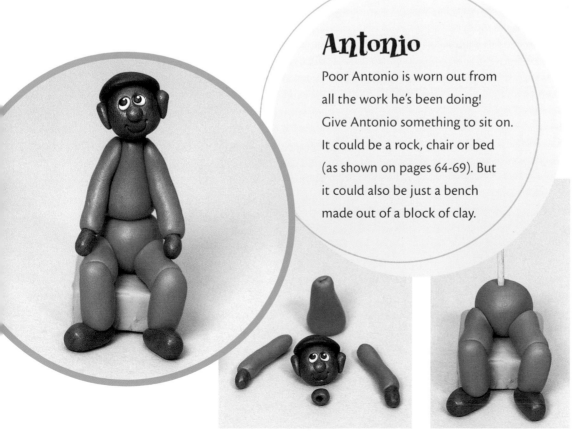

Large Characters

To help larger clay characters bake adequately, without burning or cracking, use a foil armature. A good rule of thumb to use is if your character has any parts thicker than a 1" (2cm) circle, it would be best to use a foil armature.

Greg

Meet Greg, one of the characters that I imagine in my clay world. He loves music, video games, jumping on the trampoline and playing basketball.

You can follow the steps for making Greg, but turn him into one of the characters in your clay world by changing the colors or shapes of each part. Since Greg is larger than the characters on pages 41-43, you'll use a foil armature. For more information on armatures, turn to page 39.

WHAT SIZE SHOULD THE ARMATURE BE?

The armature should be about half as tall as the finished character will be, measuring from the top of his head to the bottom of his toes (if he were standing up). If you want your sculpture of Greg to be 6" (15cm) tall, then his foil armature would be about 3" (8cm) tall. If you want him to be chubby, make it kind of round. If you want him to be skinny, make the armature very narrow.

CREATING GREG

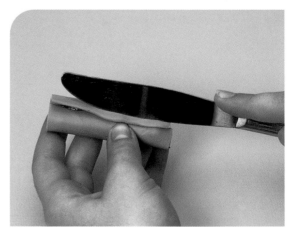

1 Start by making a foil armature of Greg's body. Roll out a sheet of flat blue clay, then cover a foil armature with the clay. Roll the clay all the way over the foil. Trim the clay where the edges meet. This is called a seam. Press and rub the seam with your fingers or thumb to "erase" it. Roll the covered armature on the table to make sure it is smooth.

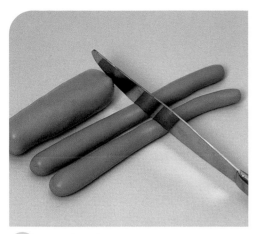

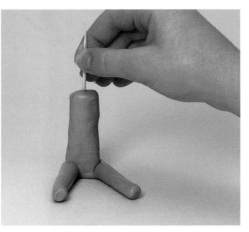

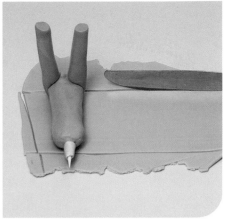

2 For this character (an average 10-
    year-old), the pantlegs are about the
same length as the body. Roll two ropes,
then cut them the same length as the body.

3 Press the pantlegs on the lower half
    of the body. Add a toothpick to the
    top of the body. For the neck, add a
small ball of flesh-colored clay.

4 To create the shirt, flatten a
    sheet of clay to approximately
    ⅟₁₆" (1cm) thick. Lay the body on
top of the clay, and cut a shirt piece as
long as the body and wide enough to
wrap around the body. The shape is a
little wider at the bottom.

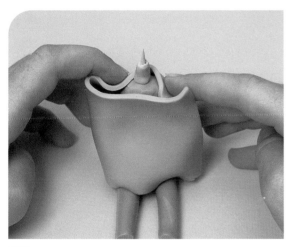

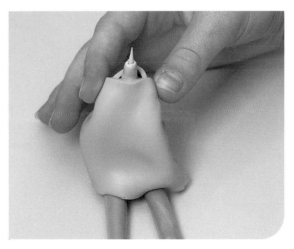

5 Join the seam of the shirt by laying one
    edge over the other to create a tube shape.
    Place the shirt over the body. Press the
back edge of the shirt around the neck.

6 Press the front shoulder edge over the body.
    Press the sides of the shirt close to the body,
    wrapping the extra clay toward the back.

Try the shirt on the
character like you would a real
shirt in the store. If it is too big, cut off
some clay. If it is too small, add some clay
and flatten it again. You might also want
to make a pattern out of paper and save it
for the next character. Remember, if you
make a bigger armature, you'll need
a bigger pattern.

tip

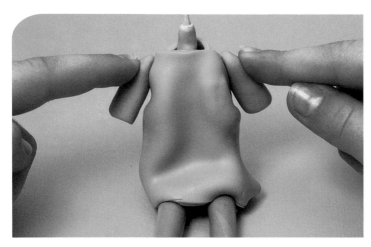

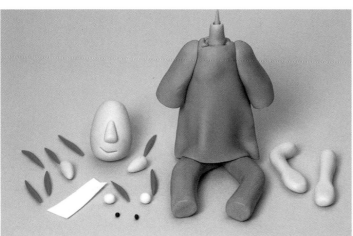

7 Make two short cylinders for the sleeves. Press them both to the body at the same time. Trim the bottom of the shirt if necessary.

8 For arms, make two long drumstick shapes. The arms, including the shirt sleeves, should reach just below the top of his legs. Flatten the end of the drumsticks slightly for hands. Press the arms against the sleeve. Create the face, adding flattened football shapes for hair. If you need help creating the face, refer to pages 26-35.

9 Add flattened eggs for shoes. Bake Greg following the directions on the package of clay.

Once you have the basic shape of the figure, try a variety of colors or facial expressions. Look at the people you see in the world around you for inspiration.

tip

HOLDING OBJECTS

The easiest way to have a clay character hold something is to wedge it in their hands, or wrap the hands tight around the object before baking. If you would like to make something for Greg to hold, such as a hamburger or basketball, turn to pages 63 and 72.

Sally

This is Sally, Greg's mother. I made her a little larger than Greg so she would look like his mother. Be careful when you make the foil armature, as it is very easy to make it too big. When I am making a family, sometimes I'll make all the armatures first. That way I can compare sizes.

Sally will sit over the edge of a shelf or on a little chair or bench.

CREATING SALLY

1 Start Sally by creating a foil armature as you did for Greg on page 44. Sally's shirt and pants are the same color. Cover the foil armature with clay. Create pantlegs from short cylinders. Make her legs using a rope of clay with a quick turn (see page 49) for her knees. Flatten one side of a drumstick for each shoes.

2 Sally is wearing a vest, made from flattened clay wrapped around her body. The top corners are turned down to make a collar. Her arms and face are made very similar to Greg's on page 46, except she has no sleeves. Place the body on the aluminum foil chair, then press all the parts together in this order: pantlegs, legs, shoes, vest, arms, neck and head. Add hair as the final step.

CREATING A SEAT

Sally needs something to sit on while you create her character, and a seat while she is baking in the oven. Wad up a piece of aluminum foil until it is the size of a bench or chair, and then create her using the seat. Once she is baked, you can move her around so she can sit in different places.

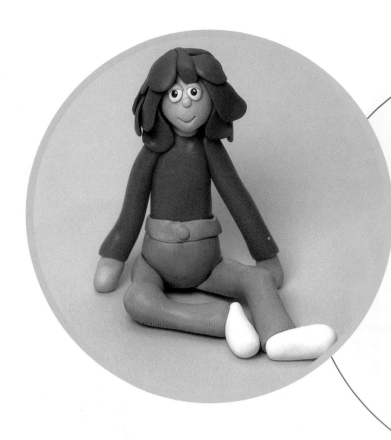

Lolly

Meet Greg's sister, Lolly. In my imagination I see her collecting and playing with the same things that I do. She collects stuffed animals because her brother Greg is allergic to real ones. If you turn to page 76, you will learn to make some of her favorite stuffed animals.

Lolly's armature is covered with the same clay that will become her shirt. You'll use a lot of what you learned making Greg on page 44 to make Lolly.

CREATING LOLLY

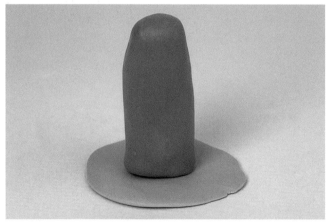

1 Create a foil armature. Wrap the foil armature with the same color clay as what Lolly's shirt will be. Choose a color of clay for her pants, and make a flat pancake with it. Set Lolly's body on the pancake.

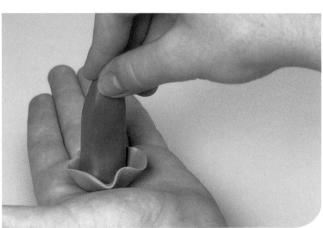

2 Press the pancake up around Lolly's waist. Use a knife to trim the clay if it is ragged, so you have a smooth line of clay that will be the top of Lolly's pants. Make sure the pancake of clay is smooth against the body.

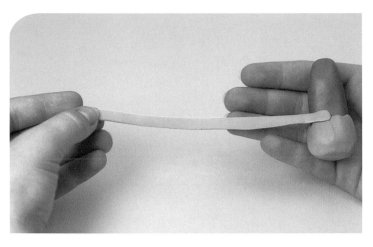

3 Create a belt by flattening a rope of clay. Wrap the belt around Lolly's waist. Trim the end.

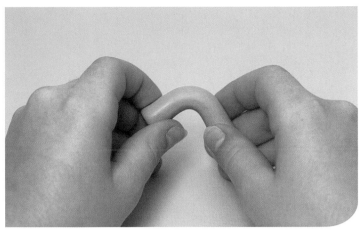

4 Roll a rope of clay for each leg. Bend the clay gently at the knees using a quick turn. See the tip below for help on making a quick turn.

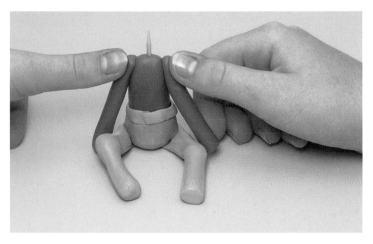

5 Press the legs onto the body. Roll two ropes for arms and press them against the shoulder. Press both at the same time to keep from getting fingerprints on other parts of the body.

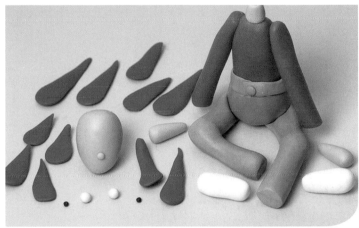

6 Make slightly flattened egg shapes for shoes, flattened teardrop shapes for ears, an egg for her head and balls for the nose and eyes. Press all the parts in place, adding the hair last. When adding the hair, start at the sides and back of the head. Add the top and bangs last.

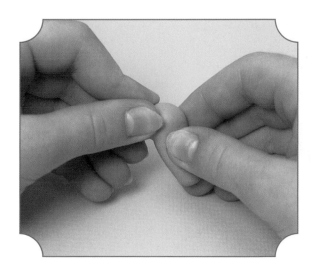

QUICK TURN

To create a knee, do a simple trick called a quick turn. Bend the clay leg, holding the knee with one hand on either side of the bend. Your fingers should be on top of the clay, not underneath. Gently press towards the center of the knee with your fingers to give the knee definition and make the clay bulge slightly.

Fred

This is Fred, Greg and Lolly's dad. Fred wakes up early in the morning and takes his dog, Max, for a run. Then he gets the paper and sits on the back porch to read. He must work at home, since we never see him leave. I think he writes books. What jobs do the people in your imaginary world do?

CREATING FRED

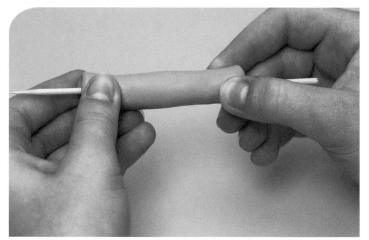

1 Begin making Fred with a foil armature (as you made for Greg on page 44). Cover the armature with a flattened sheet of clay the same color as the pants. For each leg, make a rope of clay that is slightly longer than the foil armature. Cut two bamboo skewers that are 1" (3cm) longer than the legs. Press the skewers through the legs. Leave about ½" (1cm) of the skewer sticking out on both ends.

NOTE TO ADULTS

If you can't find a bamboo skewer for this project, use a piece of coat hanger wire. Make sure you supervise the child while working with the wire. Wire can be sharp and dangerous if not used properly.

2 Use a toothpick to press two holes into the bottom of the armature where the legs will be. Then press one end of the skewers into the body.

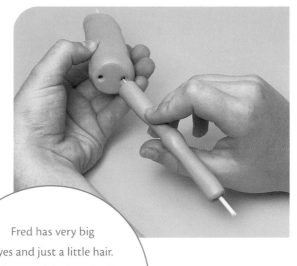

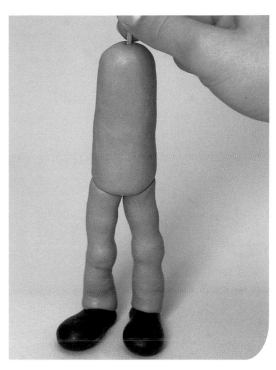

Fred has very big eyes and just a little hair. Experiment with changing how your character looks by adding different hair or changing the size of the eyes and nose.

tip

3 Press the other end of the leg skewers into shoes, which are two slightly flattened egg shapes. Pinch the shoe just slightly in front of the heel to narrow the back of the shoe. Make sure the shoes are flat and the figure stands. See page 37 for more shoes you can make.

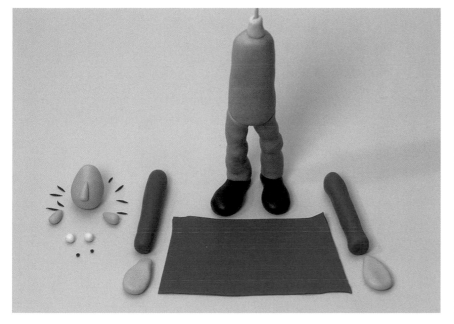

4 Make a shirt, sleeves, hands, head and hair for Fred as you did for Greg on pages 44-46. The hands are flattened ovals, the shirt is a sheet of clay and the sleeves are ropes. The head is an egg shape. Use the techniques on pages 26-35 to create a face for Fred.

5 To bake Fred, prop him between two old ceramic coffee mugs to keep him from tipping over in the oven. Follow the baking directions on the package of clay.

Making real people in clay

It's fun to make clay characters of real people. It's even more fun if you remember that the clay people don't have to look *exactly* like the real people. If you choose colors for hair, skin, eyes and clothes that are the same as the real people, then everyone will get the *idea* of who it is. The resemblance will be even closer if you look carefully at the real person to see the shape of their body and head, then try to make that shape in clay.

   Another thing to remember when making a caricature (a fun character that resembles a real person) is to exaggerate things that are special about that person. For instance, if a person has lots of hair, give your clay character even more hair. Or is someone has freckles, give them lots of freckles.

CREATING CLAY MAUREEN

This is me. I am a Storyclay™ Teller, so I chose to make myself wearing my costume. It is a unique costume, so people who see the clay character will get the clue right away that this is me! The little glasses are made of wire that was bent around a paintbrush handle to keep the circles round. The walking stick is a real stick.

CREATING CLAY SAMMY

Sammy has very blond hair and lots of energy. So I chose to emphasize his light hair and fun grin. The hardest thing about making Sammy was getting the toothpicks into his legs and still making the clay look smooth, like legs. I also paid attention to how long the legs were in relationship to his body. If I made the legs too long, Sammy would look much older.

CREATING CLAY NORA

Nora's shirt, freckles and hair make her clay character easy to recognize. To make her shirt, I cut out the pieces, then added the black lines for the smiling face. After that, I put the two halves of the shirt together and slipped it over her neck. In order to get her smooth hair just right, I made the clay character all except for the hair, then baked it. After cooling, I added the hair and baked the character again. Her freckles were added with a toothpick tip that was dipped in brown acrylic paint.

imagine the things in your world

What sort of things do you imagine in your clay world? In the last chapter we added people, but what other things do you see? Let's look at the details. Are there sports events happening? Are there animals? If there are animals, are they real or imaginary? What kinds of food do the people eat? Or do they never eat at all? Is your imaginary clay world very similar to your own, or is it very different? How is it the same, and what makes it different?

In the next section of this book, you'll learn some tricks for making a wide variety of clothing. You will find that changing the color and style of the clothing will make your characters look almost like different characters. One new thing that you'll learn in this section is how to make clay clothing with hollow pant legs and sleeves. Your clay people will look like they are really wearing their clothes, rather than just having them stuck together.

Finally, we'll take a look at some of the really crazy things you can create with your clay characters. It's time to pull out your imagination and let it take over for a while!

Creating clay clothing

Making clay clothing for characters is a bit like working with actual fabric and a sewing machine to make our own clothes. To make clay clothes, cut out pieces of clay very similar to the way you would cut out pieces of fabric.

To get ideas for clay clothing, I use real clothing as a guide. I find a shirt, dress or jacket I like, then copy the shapes of the fabric pieces in clay. In this section you'll learn lots of techniques for making clothing. Once you learn the basic steps, you can become a clay fashion designer and design your own clothing!

Hats

Hats are really fun to make as there is no limit to what can go on a hat!

Add a hat to your character and you can change the character's personality. Hats give clues about who the characters are or what they like. Look at all of these different kinds of hats. What other clay hats can you imagine?

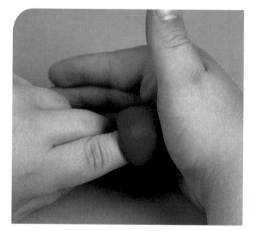

BASEBALL HAT

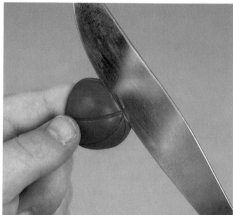

1 Roll a ball. Press a large, blunt tool into the center of the ball. Roll the tool back and forth against your work surface. When the hole is even all the way around, smooth and round the top against your finger.

2 Use a dull knife to mark in the lines in the top of the hat.

3 To make the bill for a cap, flatten an oval, then cut off one side. Roll a small ball for the top of the hat. Press all the pieces together.

TOP HAT

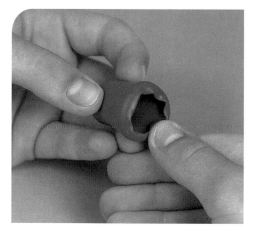

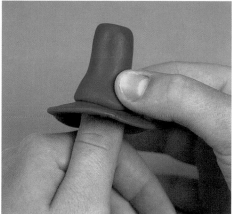

2 To make a brim for the top hat, flatten a ball of clay and press a hole through the center. Set the crown on the brim and press together. Stretch as needed to fit the character's head.

1 For the top, or crown, of the hat, roll a cylinder. Hollow it as you did the top of the baseball hat. Turn the edges into the hat.

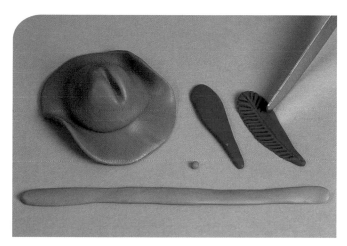

← COWBOY HAT

Begin the same as for the top hat, except make the crown from a very short cylinder. Press a tool across the top of the hat to indent. Roll up the sides of the hat. The ribbon is a flattened rope. The feather is a flattened teardrop with lines carved with a dull knife. Lay the ribbon around the hat. Press on the feather with a tiny clay ball that will look like a button.

SUN BONNET

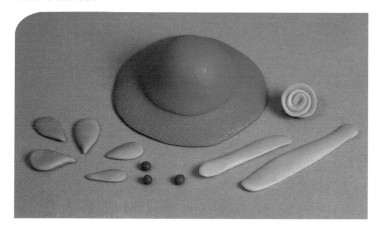

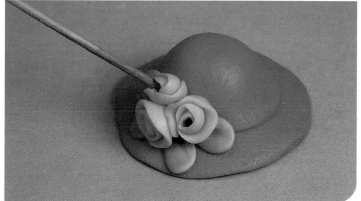

1 To make a sun bonnet, make a flat brim and a hollow crown, as you did for the top hat. Make flattened teardrops for leaves, flattened ropes for roses. To make a rose, roll up a flattened rope, then pinch the bottom slightly. Use your finger to slightly roll over the top edges of the rose.

2 Use a toothpick to press the leaves onto the hat, and then use a toothpick to pick up the roses and press them in place.

Dresses and skirts

Making dresses is very similar to making shirts, but there are a few differences, such as adding a waist. Shirts, skirts and dresses all start with a flattened piece of clay. You can use your hand, a roller, a rolling pin or have an adult use a pasta machine to flatten the clay.

WRINKLES

This character, Linda, looks older than other characters in this book because she has more lines in her face. They can be one of the clues that tell us the age of a person. To make wrinkles around the eyes, roll a skinny needle against the corners of the eyes. The lines between her chin and nose also make her look older. If you make the line shorter and curve it, it will look more like a smile line. You may want to smooth the lines with your finger to make them look softer. This is especially true if you are making someone you know!

CREATE A DRESS

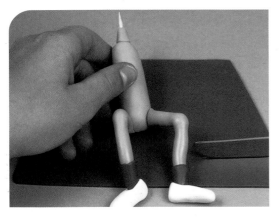

1 To judge the amount of clay you will need for the dress, lay the body armature on top of the flattened clay and cut the length you will need. For the width, cut dress about four times as wide as the body. The clay "fabric" should be cut narrower at the top than at the bottom. This keeps the clothing from being too bulky.

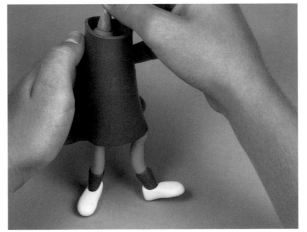

2 Overlap the dress edges, then press them together. Put the dress on over the neck of the character. The seam can be at the side, in the front or in the back. You may want to add buttons to the dress before you put it on your character.

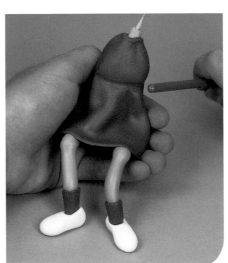

3 At the neck, press the extra clay around the shoulders, just as you did for making a shirt on page 45. Use a flat tool to make the waist area flatter.

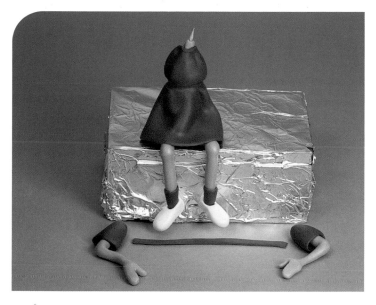

4 Hollow out two short cylinders for sleeves. Press arms into sleeves. Flatten a long rope for the belt.

5 Wrap a belt around the waist. Trim the end if it is too long. Press the sleeves and arms to the shoulders. Add a head and finish the details of the character.

CREATE A SKIRT

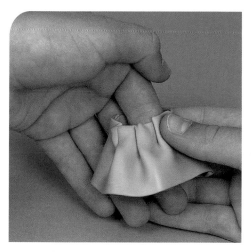

1 To make a skirt, lay your clay character on top of a piece of flattened clay. Decide how long the skirt should be. Cut a piece of clay wide enough to fit around your character at least twice, unless you are planning to make a very tight skirt! Press gathers into the top of the skirt.

2 Place the skirt over the character's neck and down onto the body. Press around the waist, then position the legs. Arrange the skirt folds to look like a real skirt. Add a shirt or blouse, then add sleeves and arms.

3 Add the head and position the character. This character will be sitting down. Putting her onto a box for baking will keep her legs in the right position for sitting. After she is baked, she can be removed from her foil-covered box and placed somewhere else.

Pants

You learned how to make basic pants in the last chapter, but sometimes it's fun to make a character with hollow pant legs into which you can put the ankle or sock. This makes the character look real, as if it could take the clothing on and off.

CREATE LONG PANTS

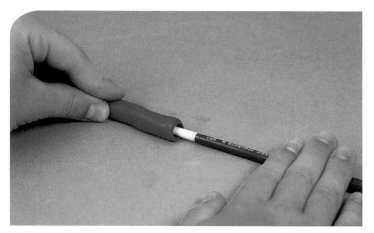

1 To make long pants, make a clay rope for each leg. Press a blunt tool halfway into the rope. Hollow out the pant leg by rolling the tool against the clay, just as you did for the hat crown on page 56.

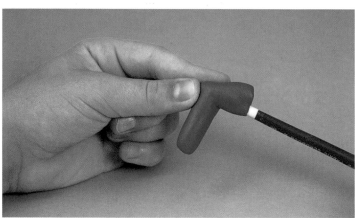

2 To make the knee, insert a blunt tool halfway into the leg and bend the knee over the tool. Be careful not to push the tool through the knee.

3 Press the pant legs onto the body, then insert the feet into the hollow pant leg. Press the pant leg together slightly to hold the foot in place.

⟵ SHORTS

Shorts are made the same way as long pants, just shorter! Start with a very short cylinder and hollow it out. Press it in place on the character's body. Add legs with a knee into the shorts. Press the pant leg against the leg to hold the legs in place.

It is easy to change the style of shirts, pants and jackets by changing the color and the decorations. Think of all of the ways you can dress up your characters by adding pockets, patches or clay buttons and beads!

tip

Special clothes

You can add layers of clay to your characters just like real people add layers of clothing. Do the people in your clay world wear suits, coats, long gowns or sports uniforms?

The clothes and accessories that you choose for your clay characters will give an impression about who they are and what kinds of things they like to do. I'm guessing, just by looking at this character, that he likes to fish, that his boots got wet, and that he is a cowboy. I'll call him Tom. I might be wrong in my guess, but at least it is fun to pretend to know his story.

ADDING A JACKET ⬆

This character is wearing a jacket that has fringes and pockets. It is easier to add these special details while the piece of clay is still flat. The fringe was cut with a knife. The pockets are just flat pieces of clay. Directions for making the hat are on page 57. By placing him on the rock for baking, you will be sure that he will fit just right. You can also make a "fake" rock as shown on page 64.

CREATING A FISHING POLE

Here's another picture of Tom, but now he is sitting on the clay rock, and he has a fishing pole. It is easy to make a fishing pole from a stick, a string and a bent piece of wire. The wire in the picture is an eyepin that is used to make jewelry, but you could just bend a piece of plain wire. I pressed the pole in his hands before he was baked.

Uniforms and sports stuff

Imagine making a personalized gift for a friend or relative who plays on a specific sports team. You could make a character that looks like her or him, and have it wearing the team's uniform. You can't buy that kind of gift in a store!

On pages 58-61, you saw how to make basic dresses, skirts, pants, shirts and jackets. Now let's talk about adding extra little details to turn that basic clothing into a uniform. I could make a character like this one for my friend Jeff, who loves playing baseball. Outfield is his favorite position.

CREATING A UNIFORM ⬆

Words and numbers can be added to the front of the shirt by making little ropes and pressing them in place in the clay. Use little ropes to add a letter to the front of the hat as well. Directions for making the baseball hat can be found on page 56. The shirt is assembled the same way the shirt is on page 46.

ADDING EQUIPMENT

Look on page 63 to learn how to make sports equipment. You can easily add equipment to your clay characters' hands to give them some personality. Details tell us what the characters like to do.

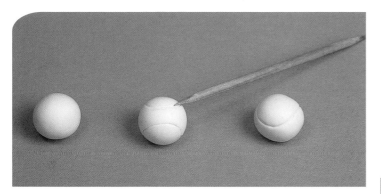

SOFTBALL OR BASEBALL

Roll a white ball, then use a toothpick to draw lines where the two parts of a real baseball are sewn together. The easiest way to do this is to get a real baseball or softball and look closely at the shape of the lines, then copy that shape.

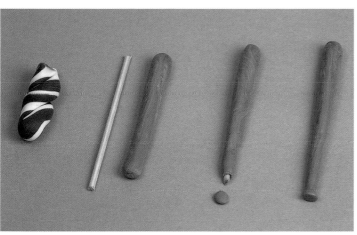

BAT

Mix together white and light brown clay, but don't completely mix the clay. Roll a rope, then press a toothpick into the center. Roll and stretch the clay until the toothpick is covered and the clay is smooth. Make one end blunt and round, and the other end skinny. Press a small ball to the skinny end of the bat.

BASKETBALL

Roll a ball of clay. Add a foil center if the ball will be thicker than 1" (3cm). Smooth the ball, then create a line around the basketball. Turn the ball and carve between the first set of lines. This divides the basketball into four equal parts. Add more stitching lines as needed.

FOOTBALL

1 To make a football, start with a round ball of clay. If the football is more than 1" (3cm) wide, add a foil ball to the center. A larger ball with a foil center will bake more evenly. Shape the clay into a basic football shape.

2 Use a knife to carve a line lengthwise around the middle of the football. Turn the football and carve once more around the middle, carving between the first lines. This divides the football into four equal parts. For lacing, roll a skinny white rope. Carve rope into short pieces and lay them on the ball. Press seam lines around the lacing.

Making things in your world

Anything you see in the real world can be copied and made into a tiny clay version of the real thing. In this section of the book I will show you how to make some things, such as chairs, beds, food and toys. Once you learn the basic steps for creating each of these things, you can use what you've learned, plus your imagination, to make many more things for your clay world. If you start running out of ideas, pick up a toy catalog, a picture book or a magazine and look at some of the things in the pictures. Have fun!

Rocks

You can use real rocks as chairs for your characters, but they are kind of heavy. It's fun to mix colors to make pretend rocks. With polymer clay you can make them look so real!

1 To make rocks, choose colors of polymer clay that you might find in real rocks. Mix and twist the colors together as you did in color mixing on page 10. If you don't mix your clay up all the way, you can give it a mottled appearance like real stone.

CREATING A ROCK

2 When you have the clay mixed into a fun color, use a roller to flatten it to the thickness of thin cardboard. Wad foil up to look like a rock shape. Be sure you have a flat spot on the foil rock where your character can sit. Lay the foil on top of the flattened sheet of clay.

3 Wrap the clay sheet around the foil, then smooth any seams with your finger. The rock on the left is a clay rock; the one on the right is a real rock. Push a real rock against the clay rock to give it a rock-like texture, and then bake the clay rock following the package directions.

Wooden chairs

This clay chair looks like real wood! To make a smaller chair, start the same as for the larger chair, but with a smaller foil armature. For small chairs, use toothpicks in the legs; for larger ones, use wood skewers.

Make clay look like wood by twisting together several shades of beige and brown. Roll the clay mix into a log shape, then cut the log in half, stack it and roll again. Keep doing this until the color mix looks like wood. Flatten the clay, then check the color again. You can always remix by adding a darker or lighter color if you don't like your first results.

tip

MAKING A WOODEN CHAIR

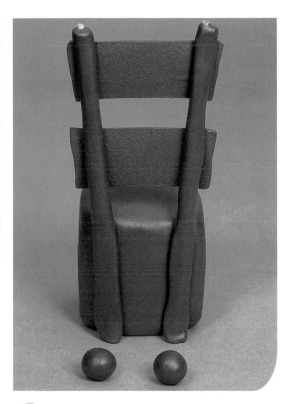

1 Roll a sheet of foil into a ball, then flatten the sides to make a cube. Lay the foil cube on a sheet of flattened brown clay, then cut the clay to cover the sides of the cube. It should look like a plus (+) sign. You'll need one more clay square for the last side. Cover the foil cube and smooth the corners.

2 Cut two wood skewers the same height as the chair. Roll two clay ropes. Press a skewer into the center of the rope, then stretch and roll the clay along the skewer. To make slats for the chair back, cut two strips that are as wide, or slightly wider, than the chair seat from a flattened piece of clay.

3 Press two clay-covered skewers to the back of the seat. Press the two slats in place between the skewers. Roll two balls, then press them to the top of the chair.

Comfy chairs

Place your clay characters on this comfy clay chair instead of just a rock or shelf. You might even copy the shape and colors of your favorite chair. Just bend the foil into the shape of the chair, then use the colors of clay to match the chair.

THE UPHOLSTERED CHAIR

1 Wad up a piece of foil into a loose ball, then flatten the sides until it resembles a chair seat. You can add or remove foil if the ball looks too big or small. To make the back of the chair, fold, shape and smooth four layers of foil into a long, flat shape. Compare it to your chair seat to see if it resembles a seat back.

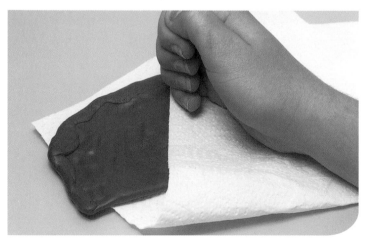

2 Flatten the clay until it's very thin, about 1⁄16" (1cm). Lay the foil chair back on the clay sheet, and cut a clay piece large enough to cover both sides of foil. Be sure to cut the clay edges slightly larger than the foil edges. Cover both sides of the foil with clay. Press the clay edges together, then press the clay-covered chair back with cloth or a paper towel to add texture.

Sometimes air gets trapped between layers of clay, forming bubbles. To help cover up the bubbles, texturize the clay surface by pressing it with a rough cloth. You can remove air by slicing through the bubble, then pressing the air out. You can also try to press the bubble towards the edge of the clay so that it can escape.

tip

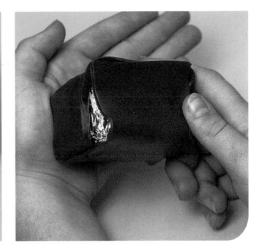

3 Lay the foil chair seat on a sheet of flattened clay. The clay will need to be four times as wide as the foil in order to cover all four sides. Use the foil to measure how wide that will be by turning it four times across the clay sheet.

4 Cut the clay piece to cover the sides of the foil seat. The middle piece should wrap around the foil, and the ends over the top. The clay shape will look like a big letter "T".

5 Fold the clay over the foil. Press the edges together, then press with fabric to add texture.

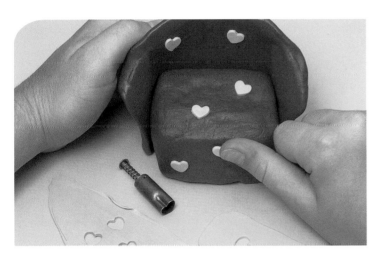

6 Press the clay-covered back to the seat. Flatten a small piece of several different colors of clay. Use a cutter or a knife to cut out the shapes. Press the shapes to the chair. Bake the finished chair, following the directions on the package of clay.

DIFFERENT SIZES!

These chairs were made in the same way. They started with different sizes of foil armatures. Match the size of your chair to the clay people that you are making. Do you want them to look like little people in big chairs, or average-sized people in average chairs?

Beds

If you were to design a clay bed for your clay characters, what would it look like? What color would it be? What would be on top of the bed, or beside it?

To make the armature for the mattress and box springs, roll a sheet of foil into a ball, then flatten the sides the same as you did for the chair on page 66. This time the foil needs to be a flat rectangle, and it needs to be very, very smooth. If it's not smooth, the bedspread will look lumpy, just like a messy bed. To make the foil smooth, press it firmly against your work surface. Check the size of the foil "mattress" with your little clay people, and change the size if you need to.

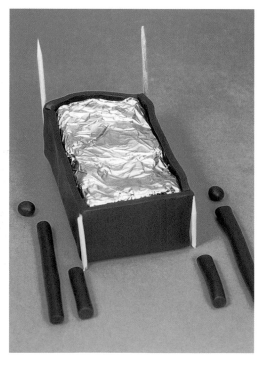

MAKING A BED

1 Mix clay for the colors that you will need for the bed and the bedspread. Twist and fold the clay until it is finely striped. Flatten it to see if the clay is striped.

I kept the bed on a piece of paper while I worked. This allowed me to turn the bed easily without having to touch it and get fingerprints all over it.

tip

2 Lay the foil "mattress" on a sheet of flattened clay, and cut out a section of clay that covers the bottom and the four sides of the foil. You don't need to cover the top of the foil. Fold the sides of the clay over the foil and smooth the edges.

3 Measure toothpicks for the four bed posts. You can make them any height you want, and even match the shape of your own bed. Cover the toothpicks or skewers with clay ropes. Press them firmly to the sides of the bed, then press balls of clay onto the top of the headboard for posts.

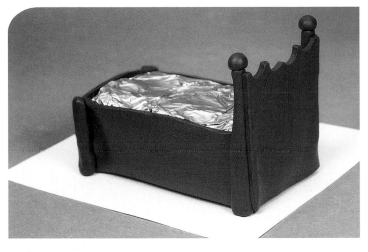

4 Cut a piece of flat clay to fit between the two headboard posts. Decorate the top with a design if you like, using a cut straw as a cutting shape. Press the headboard between the two headboard posts.

5 To make a pillow, fold a piece of paper towel into a pillow shape. Tape the sides together. Flatten a sheet of clay, then cover the pillow and smooth the edges.

6 Flatten clay for the sheet and bedspread. For the sheet, cut a narrow piece of clay that stretches from one side of the bed to the other. Cut a piece for the bedspread. It should be as wide as the sheet, and long enough to fit from the top of the bed to the end.

7 Lay the sheet, then the bedspread over the foil mattress and bed. Position the folds as desired. Place pillow on bed and bake according to directions on package of clay.

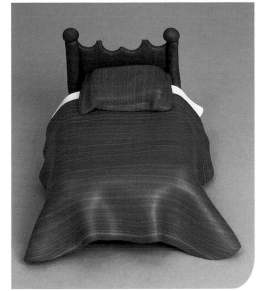

MAKING A BED BOX

It is easy to make this project into a hidden treasure box if you follow these steps:

1. Be sure that the clay at the corners of the bed is loose from the foil. Stick a toothpick into the corners to lift the clay away from the foil. Bake bed frame for 20 minutes. Let cool.

2. Make the bedspread strong enough to lift off bed. Roll the clay for the bedspread a little thicker.

3. Press the sheet to the bedspread.

4. Brush cornstarch or baby powder over the bottom of the clay pieces to keep them from sticking to the baked bed frame. Place the bedspread on the bed.

5. Bake the bed and let it cool. When you lift off the bedspread and sheet and remove the foil armature, you'll have an empty space inside the bed.

Tables

You can decide how tall and how big you want your table to be. The table is built over a foil cylinder. Check the height of the cylinder against some of your clay characters. To change the height, press the foil against your work surface to make it shorter. If it is too short, add more foil. Do the same thing with the cardboard circle that is the top of the table. You can always cut a bigger or smaller circle.

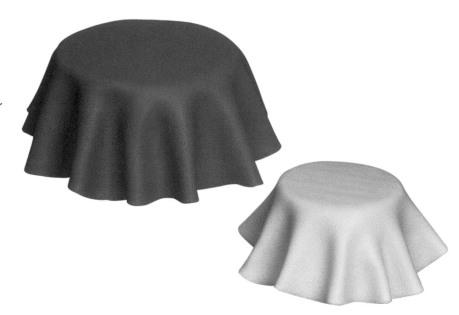

MAKING A TABLE

1 Roll a sheet of foil into a ball, then flatten two sides to make a cylinder. To make a tabletop, use a cup or circle pattern to draw a circle on a piece of cardboard. Cut out the circle.

To decide how wide the circle of clay should be for the tablecloth, use a piece of string to measure the distance from your work surface to the cardboard tabletop, across the top of the table, and then back down the other side.

tip

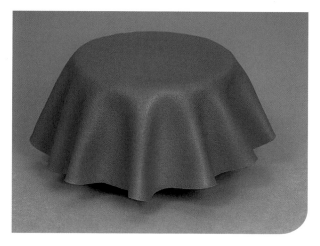

2 Cover the bottom half of the foil cylinder with a sheet of clay. Press the clay firmly to the foil. Use thick white glue to fasten the cardboard circle to the top of the foil cylinder. Let the glue dry.

3 For the tablecloth, roll a sheet of clay, then cut a circle the size you will need to cover the table. Lay the circle of clay over the cardboard base. To make the clay look like fabric, pull it down over the edge of the cardboard, then use your fingers to gently press in folds. Bake the table according to the instructions on the package of clay.

Food

In this section, I've chosen some of my favorite foods to make in clay, but it's easy to make changes. Change the colors of clay and you will change the recipes. The apple might be yellow instead of red. Or change it into a pear or a plum! Make a hamburger into a chicken sandwich by using beige clay instead of brown, or leave the cheese out of the sandwich if you like.

MAKE AN APPLE

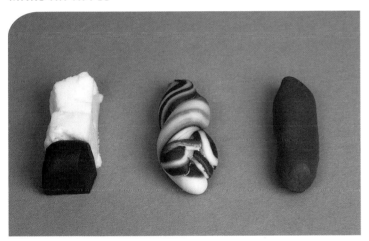

1 Mix translucent polymer clay with red, yellow or green clay to make an apple color. A mix of half translucent clay to half colored clay will make the apple skin look more real.

2 Roll the clay into a ball shape, then into an egg. Flatten both ends slightly. Make indentations in the top and bottom of the apple. From brown clay, roll a tiny ball to press into the bottom of the apple and to add a short stem for the top. Add a highlight color to the apple by brushing on some chalk or makeup that is a slightly darker color than your apple.

FOOD FOR THOUGHT

Add some food to your clay characters' hands, such as a sandwich, and they will seem to come even more alive.

MAKE A SANDWICH!

1 To make bread for your sandwiches, start with the shape of the bread. For a hamburger bun, roll a ball of white clay, then flatten it slightly. Create a pile of chalk dust by coloring hard with brown chalk on a piece of paper. Mix colors of chalk if you like. Use a brush to "paint" chalk dust onto the bun. This makes the crust look like it was baked.

2 Decide what you would like to put into your clay sandwich. To make cheese, lettuce, tomatoes, roast beef, salami and a hamburger, look on this page at sandwich fixings.

3 To build the sandwich, slice the bun open, just as you would a real bun. A dull knife may flatten the bun. You may need to ask an adult to use a sharp knife to cut it. Pile on the meat and vegetables. Put the halves back together and bake.

MAKE A SUB! ⬆

To make a sub sandwich, roll a ball of clay into a long oval shape and flatten it slightly. Finish the sandwich the same way as the hamburger, except add roast beef and salami along with the vegetables and cheese. Of course, you can add anything you like, as long as you ask the clay people who will be eating it!

SANDWICH FIXINGS

Here's an easy way to make food for your sandwich. Mix translucent clay with colored clay to create the colors for each item. Leave the colors partially mixed, as it will look more real. Roll each item into a log, except for the hamburger.

Lettuce will look real if you flatten and stretch the green clay so that it is very thin. Pull at the edges to make it look torn.

For salami, mix a little white and red clay in with brown clay. Leave it partially mixed.

For hamburger, flatten a ball of brown clay. Press it with an old toothbrush to give it a rough texture.

You can use small slices of colored clay to make fixings like cheese, tomatoes and pickles.

MAKE A PIZZA

1 Mix translucent clay with a tiny piece of brown clay to make a dough color. Roll the clay into a ball, then flatten it to resemble a pizza crust. Press the middle of the crust to make the edges thicker than the middle. Brush brown chalk on the clay to "bake" the crust.

2 To make tomato sauce, mix a small amount of red clay into translucent clay. Roll it into a ball, then flatten and press it in place so that it covers the bottom of the crust. Cut small slices of the salami and lay them on top of the sauce. Press yellow clay through the garlic press to make it look like grated cheese, and add it on the crust. Brush the cheese with brown chalk

MAKE SPAGHETTI

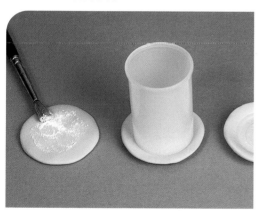

2 To make spaghetti, mix a little white clay with translucent clay. Make long strands with a garlic press and lay the strands on the dish. To make meatballs, roll tiny brown clay balls. Press with a toothbrush for texture.

1 To make a plate, roll a ball of clay. Flatten the ball and brush with powder or cornstarch. Press a circular tool into the center of the clay to make an inner circle.

Lay the spaghetti plate on a piece of paper while you are working so that it won't stick to your work surface.

tip

3 Bake the clay according to the package directions. When the clay is cool, mix a little red paint into white glue for sauce. Drip it over spaghetti and meatballs. Let it dry.

Cars

Clay people may need cars, too! How about this orange car? It would be easy to create a car in another color and style. How about making it two-toned?

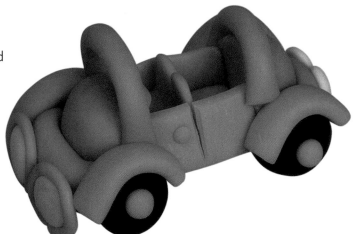

BUILDING A CAR

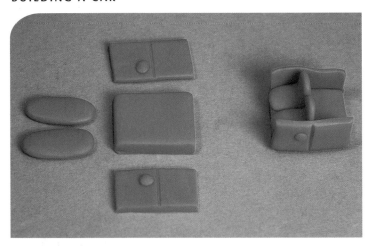

1 This picture shows the center part of the car. The larger square is the floor of the car. The size of this piece will determine the size of the car. For each seat, make two small ovals, then flatten them. Press one end of each oval to the car floor, then bend up the other end to make the back of the seat. For the doors, make two rectangles that are as long as the car floor, but not as wide. Use a knife or toothpick to press a line along each door. Add a small ball for each door handle. Press the parts together.

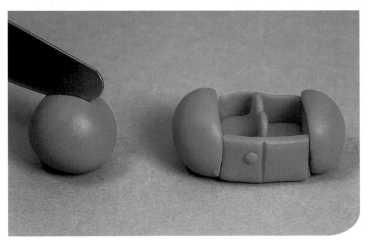

2 To make the front and back of the car, roll a large ball. Cut it in half, then press one half against the front of the car and the other against the back. If the size isn't right, roll another ball and try again.

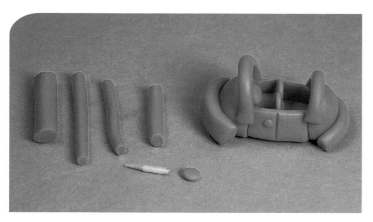

3 Roll a thick rope for the front bumper, and a thinner one for the top of the window. Roll a short rope for the trim behind the seats, and another rope for the back bumper. Make a steering wheel from a small toothpick with a flattened ball placed on top. Press the steering wheel in place first, then press on the other pieces.

4 Make a support for your car from a crumpled piece of foil. This support will keep the weight of the car off the soft clay wheels so that they will stay round. The bottom and top of this support needs to be flat, so press it against your work surface to make it firm. It can't be wider than the body of your car. For wheels, roll four black balls. Flatten them, then roll a small ball for the center of each wheel. Set the car on the foil support, then press the parts of the wheels in place.

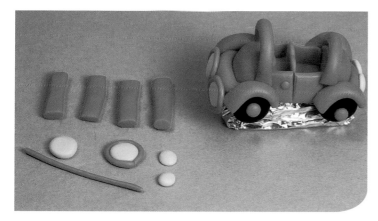

5 For fenders, roll a rope. Flatten it slightly and cut one piece for each fender. Lay a piece over each wheel. Roll two yellow balls for the headlights and two for the taillights. Flatten each slightly. Roll a rope to wrap around each headlight and press the lights in place.

MORE CARS

Make a whole fleet of cars and trucks! Stack together interesting shapes, then add wheels. If you have trouble getting started, follow the general steps used in making the orange car. These imaginary vehicles make great props for your clay characters.

Stuffed animals

Clay people need things to play with, too. Make a stuffed bear or rabbit to add to someone's lap, or make some animals to place on a clay bed or chair. Once you learn the basic steps for making a stuffed animal, try changing the colors or the size of the basic shapes. Make them look like the ones sitting on your own bed.

THE BASIC STUFFED ANIMAL

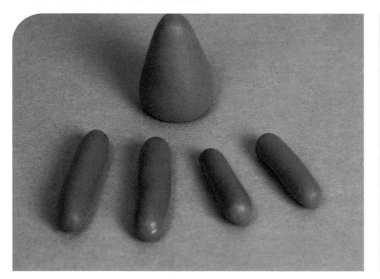

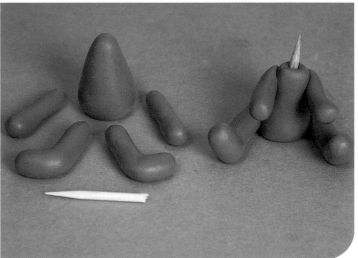

1 Make an egg shape and four short ropes. These are the beginning shapes for all the stuffed animals in the picture above. Make them in the clay color of your choice. Try different sizes, and see what works for your clay characters.

2 To shape hands and feet, do a drumstick roll (see page 17) at the wrist and ankle. Bend up the foot. Press a piece of toothpick into the neck. Press the arms and legs to the body. You have now made a body that can turn into many different animals. What makes the difference between stuffed animals is the shape of the head.

Little changes can make a big difference. For example, really big round ears on a bear will turn it into a mouse!

tip

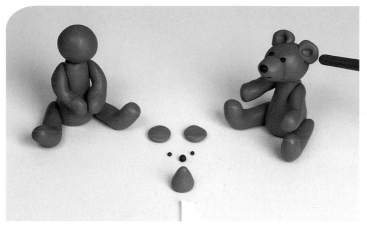

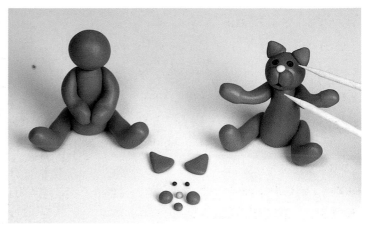

STUFFED BEAR ⬆

Roll a ball for the bear's head and set the head on a toothpick. Roll a ball for each ear, then flatten the ears. Roll a tiny black ball for each eye and a slightly bigger one for the nose. For the snout, roll a short cone. To assemble, add the snout first to the head, then the eyes, nose and ears. Press a rounded tool into each ear to fasten it to the head. To make the mouth, press a piece of cut straw into the snout (see page 20).

STUFFED CAT ⬆

Roll a ball of clay for the cat's head and set the head on a toothpick. Make a short, flattened cone shape for each ear. Roll a tiny black ball for each eye. For the cheeks and bottom lip, roll two medium-sized balls and one smaller one. For the nose, roll a small pink ball. Press all of the parts in place, starting with the ball for the bottom lip. Press a toothpick into each eye to make the pupil, and between the cheeks and lips to make an open mouth.

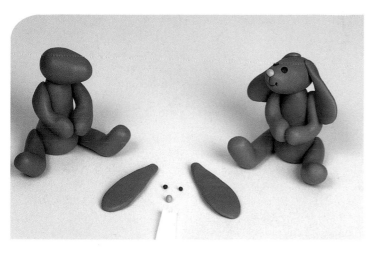

⬅ STUFFED RABBIT

To make a rabbit's head, roll a ball, then turn it into an egg. Set the head on a toothpick. Make a long, flattened teardrop shape for each ear. Roll a tiny black ball for each eye, and a slightly larger pink ball for the nose. Press the parts in place on the head. Use a cut straw to make the mouth and the line between the mouth and nose.

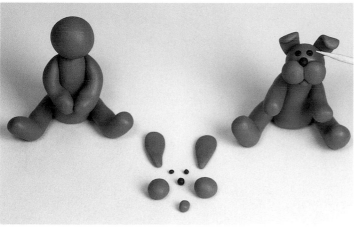

⬅ STUFFED DOG

To make a dog, roll a ball for the head, and set the head on the toothpick. Make a short, flattened teardrop shape for each ear. Roll a tiny black ball for each eye and a bigger one for the nose. For the cheeks and bottom lip, roll two medium-sized balls and one smaller one. Press all of the parts in place on the head, starting with the ball for the bottom lip. Press a toothpick into each eye to make the pupil.

Imagination time!

In this book, you've learned about polymer clay, mixing colors and ways to use tools. You've learned about shapes and putting shapes together. Now, take what you've learned, mix it all together, and come up with something new! Use your imagination to create a world that has never been seen before. Creating things from your imagination is what makes you an artist.

Imagine ...

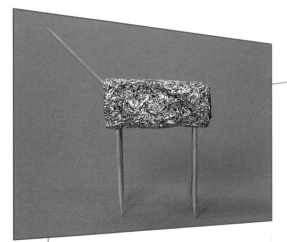

... using the armature I created for Fran the purple cow on page 13 to create a new animal.

We could use the same armature to make an orange horse. Looks like he's confused about his shoes! His tail and mane, as well as the shape of his ears and neck, make him look different from the cow.

Mix up parts from different animals, and you can create something like this "Eledorse"! His head started as a long teardrop shape. Naming your new creations is part of the fun.

imagination Time

Sometimes all it takes to change an ordinary creation into one that zings is to add a fancy hat. A long, straight wire was put inside the clay, then bent to hold the shape of the hat. The end was twisted after it was baked.

I love this "Girafanot" because he's so colorful. His tail began as a long skinny football. His horns and neck stand up so straight because of the toothpicks inside the clay.

Your imaginary world will be even more fun if you explore your imagination. People can have extra big noses, ears or feet. And they can be made in any color!

Everything in your clay world could have a story to tell! Sometimes you might create the stories. But sometimes, the clay characters seem to be telling the stories. Imagine your world in clay, and anything can happen. Have fun!

Characters in your world tell a story with the expressions on their faces. I think this little pink guy is upset because his horse won't run, or perhaps the horse is afraid to get his new shoes dirty.

Create a world of crafts with North Light Books!

CLAY CHARACTERS FOR KIDS

Mold polymer clay into a fantasy world right out of your imagination! Maureen Carlson shows you how to sculpt 10 easy shapes that can be used to create dozens of different creatures and characters, including dragons, goblins, fairies, ghosts, pigs, dogs, horses, bunnies and more.

ISBN 1-58180-286-2, paperback, 80 pages, #32161-K

STAMP YOUR STUFF

This jam-packed idea book shows readers how to create stamps from such common household items as erasers, craft foam, tape dispensers, cookie cutters and air-dry clay. Tweens and kids can make unique gifts for their family and friends with the inexpensive and easy-to-find tools and supplies for each project.

ISBN 1-58180-386-9, paperback, 64 pages, #32432-K

PAINTING ON ROCKS FOR KIDS

Hey Kids! You can create amazing creatures, incredible toys and wild gifts for your friends and family. All it takes is some paint, a few rocks and your imagination! Easy-to-follow pictures and instructions show you how to turn stones into something cool- racecars, bugs, lizards, teddy bears and more.

ISBN 1-58180-255-2, paperback, 64 pages, #32085-K

WIZARD CRAFTS

Spin a magical spell with wizards, dragons, magic potions and more! Inside you'll find 23 spellbinding projects that bring your child's imagination to life. With easy-to-follow, detailed instructions and clear photographs, you'll take a step-by-step journey into a magical adventure.

ISBN 1-58180-437-7, paperback, 96 pages, #32634-K

These and other fine imprint books are available at your local art & craft retailer, bookstore, online supplier or by calling 1-800-448-0915.